HOME AWAY FROM HOME

Janet Geringer Woititz

HEALTH COMMUNICATIONS, INC.

Janet Geringer Woititz, Ed.D.
Institute for Counseling & Training
Verona, New Jersey

Library of Congress Cataloging-in-Publication Data

Woititz, Janet Geringer.
  Home away from home.

  Bibliography: p.
  1. Alcoholism and employment — United States. 2. Children of alcoholic parents — Employment — United States. 3. Children of alcoholic
parents — United States — Psychology. I. Title.
HF5549.5.A4W65   1987   658.3'045   86-33478
ISBN 0-932194-38-9

Published by Health Communications, Inc.
Pompano Beach, Florida 33069

Dedication

This book is dedicated to my family at work who have demonstrated that through caring, awareness, hard work and commitment a healthy environment is possible.

And to my family at home who have demonstrated that through caring, awareness, hard work and commitment a healthy environment is possible.

Thanks to

Kathy Mandato
Alice Moore
Jeff Doorn
Kerry Peltier
Jim Mulhern
Mel Sandler
Bonnie White
Edye Turtz
Donald Gregg
Peter Vegso
Gary Seidler
Bernie Zweben
Dave, Lisa & Danny
Eric Wagman Photography Studios

Preface and Acknowledgments

My past writings have been a reflection of my clinical experience and have been written for CoAs and others from dysfunctional families. These books were attempts to point out and validate life experience.

This book was written with this sense of validation in mind, but also in the hopes of influencing corporate America to include these issues in their employee assistance programming. In order to do that, I have enlisted the assistance of a number of consultants (1) to verify my findings and (2) to include their own experience. I could not have accomplished this without their very able and willing assistance.

I therefore wish to acknowledge them. Since much of the material is confidential, I am limited to their names, geographic area, and specialty.

Administrative
— Gyni Garner, MSW — Charlotte, North Carolina
— Bob Lynn, NCC, CAC — Piscataway, New Jersey
— Kerry Peltier, MA, CAC — Verona, New Jersey

Professional
— Pat Clyne, BA, RN — Astoria, New York
— Kathi Goode, MA — Montclair, New Jersey
— Rev. James Mahoney, PhD — Chatham, New Jersey
— Audrey Roberts, MA — Montclair, New Jersey

Clinical
— George Brines, AAS, CAC — Lafayette, Indiana
— Dana Finnegan, PhD — South Orange, New Jersey

— Emily McNally, MA — New York City
— Martha Moore-Russell, PhD — Princeton, New Jersey
— Amy Stromsten, CAC — Cambridge, Massachusetts
— Bick Wanck, MD — Conifer Park, New York

Research
— Coleen Peruo, BA — East Rutherford, New Jersey
— Patrick Peruo, PhD — East Rutherford, New Jersey

General
— Jackson Braider, MA — New York, New York
— Ed Gogek, MD — Providence, Rhode Island
— Matt Johnson, BSW — Anchorage, Alaska
— Marlyn Stager — Hawthorne, New Jersey
— Lisa Woititz, BA — Montclair, New Jersey

Employee Assistance Programs
— Debby Bern, MSW — New Rochelle, New York
— Leighton Clark, MSW — Chicago, Illinois
— Mel Sandler, MSW — Teaneck, New Jersey
— Betty-Ann Weinstein, MSW — Washington, D.C.

Introduction

The impact of growing up with alcoholism pervades every aspect of adult life. It influences feelings of self, relationships and one's ability to get things done, regardless of whether one is looking at the home, social, or work environment.

Since a large portion of one's waking hours are spent in the workplace, whatever or wherever that setting may be, the way one feels and behaves in that environment is a significant part of one's life.

The same dynamics that cause difficulty at home may serve one in very good stead in the workplace. A secretary's family may go nuts with her compulsive need for order and attention to detail, but her boss probably values it greatly. On the other hand, your friend may be very grateful that you are driving him to work while his car is in the shop, but your supervisor may see your lateness as a hostile act.

Similar traits play out differently depending on the environment. These examples of issues — issues involving control of environment as a reaction to growing up with anarchy and the inability to say no for fear of rejection — are fairly common to children of alcoholics. This study evolved in order to satisfy my own curiosity as to how they play out in the workplace.

To the Employer:

There is little question that CoAs are among your most productive and valuable employees. They are dedicated, conscientious, capable, loyal and will do everything in their power to please.

You will find them in high management positions as well as

in unskilled jobs. These qualities are brought to whatever they do regardless of status or pay scale.

Why then, if CoAs are so desirable as employees, devote a book to their problems and encourage Employee Assistance Programs (EAPs) to pay particular attention to addressing them? Much of the reason lies in prevention.

1. CoAs are prime candidates for burnout. The excellent performance you admire and want has a limited life span.
2. CoAs tend not to know how to handle stress and lose more days due to illness than other employees.
3. CoAs are prone to depression, especially around holiday time, so performance may lag at those times.
4. CoAs have difficulty with separation and change so are prone to quit impulsively or do poorly with new opportunities.
5. CoAs run a higher risk of developing their own substance-abuse problems than other employees.

The Research Triangle Institute (RTI) estimates that the combined cost of the U.S. economy of Alcohol, Drug Abuse and Mental Illness (ADM) disorders was $197.7 billion in 1980 according to a new analysis for the Alcohol, Drug Abuse, and Mental Health Administration (ADAMHA).

In the report on *Economic Costs to Society of Alcohol and Drug Abuse and Mental Illness* (1980), RTI researchers estimated the economic costs of alcohol abuse and alcoholism in 1980 to be $89.5 billion. The projected costs of alcoholism and alcohol abuse in 1983 were $116.7 billion.

The RTI study indicates that alcohol abuse affects productivity among the general population far more than researchers had previously estimated. According to the RTI report, problem drinkers are 21% **less productive** when compared to otherwise similar persons, accounting for $49.8 billion in reduced productivity.

But "the overall prevalence rate has not changed", the authors say. "It is estimated to be **10% of the work force**."

Enlightened Employee Assistance Program (EAP) personnel are able to identify children of alcoholics' issues when they surface and as a result are able to treat many right in the work-place. More and more EAP programs are reporting large numbers of their case loads as children of alcoholics.

The bottom line is that early intervention with children of alcoholics in the workplace is cost effective.

It is also true that the models developed for identifying and treating children of alcoholics may be applied to children from other dysfunctional families as well. Many similarities exist between CoAs (children of alcoholics) and those who grew up with other compulsive behaviors such as gambling, drug abuse, overeating, those who experienced chronic illness, or were subjected to profound religious attitudes. They can also apply to those who were adopted or lived in foster care. The patterns are not exclusive, so the benefits of workplace aware-ness carry even greater significance.

To the CoA Employee:

Regardless of the degree of success that you achieve in the "world of work," there are questions that continue to plague you. These are the result of feelings that get in the way of your finding the satisfaction appropriate to your job performance or finding the courage either to assert your needs or make neces-sary changes. This is not only confusing to you but damaging to your self-image. You end up very angry at yourself. "Why do I . . . when I know better? Why don't I . . . when I know how? Why can't I accept praise? Why does criticism devastate me? Why do I sabotage success? Why am I overwhelmed so much of the time? Why is everyone else better able to cope than I? Is there any end to it? Could my parents really be responsible?" And on and on this seemingly endless list of questions goes.

This book is designed to answer questions for the CoA employee and to develop a perspective for EAP personnel to include in designing their programs. The goal is to make the work experience more satisfying for the person who has grown up in a dysfunctional system and make the work environment more effective for all concerned.

Later on in this book is an overview of the characteristics discussed in the book *Adult Children of Alcoholics* (Health Communications, 1983) and their specific impact in the workplace. Samples of different work environments and how they reflect the old life at home are included. How and why these set up a work environment that is all too reminiscent of the family of origin becomes clear.

Also included are the myths held by CoAs in the workplace and how these perpetuate a poor self-image — leading to workaholism, subsequent burnout, and the inability for many to ever get started at all.

The toxic interaction of these elements among peers and supervisors — the **inevitability** of it — will become apparent.

Ways to affect change from the point of view of the counselor, the CoA, and the corporation are dealt with in the second half of the book. It is designed to be used by both the employee assistance person as a counseling tool and by the employee for self-help.

The research component is added to reinforce the idea that, regardless of the particular occupation or the particular industry, the difficulties experienced by CoAs are similar and therefore can be treated similarly.

CONTENTS

PART ONE

ON THE JOB

Chapter One

THE CoA

One of the original assumptions in researching this book was that children of alcoholics (CoAs) are found predominantly in stressful occupations. This hypothesis was not sustained. It is apparent that CoAs are represented in all job categories. The occupational choices seemed to follow those of the general population. The charts presented in the following pages show this distribution.

The anecdotal material demonstrates that, regardless of occupational choice, the qualities inherent in being a CoA predominate. It appears that stress was created by the CoA even when it was not inherent in the job description. The CoA teacher, technician, religious worker, foreman, airline employee, administrator, nurse, athlete, soldier or officer, waitress, and medical student all have much more in common.

─────────────────── **Figure 1.0** ───────────────────

ACoA OCCUPATIONAL GROUPING (238 ACoAs)
(4 or more ACoAs in an occupation: Total of 165 ACoAs or 69%)

Counselor	17
Secretary	12
Registered Nurse	11
Small Business Owner	10
Administrator	10
Sales Representative	10
Teacher	9
Home Maker	9
Clerical Worker	8
Accountant	8
Manager	7
Social Worker	7
Student	6
Self Employed	6
Health Technicians	5
Commercial Writer	4
Bookkeeper	4
Engineer	4
Librarian	4
Lawyer	4
Bus Driver	4
Credit Rep/Mgr	4
Others 3 or less ACoAs	73 ACoAs or 31%

─────────── **Figure 1.1** ───────────

MALE ACoA OCCUPATIONAL GROUPING (64 MALE ACoAs)
(3 or more male ACoAs in an occupation: Total of 33 or 52%)

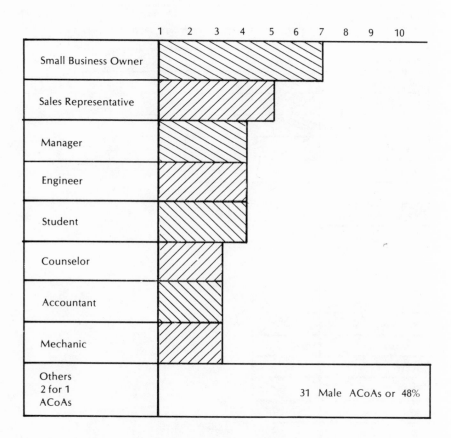

---------------------- **Figure 1.2** ----------------------

FEMALE ACoA OCCUPATIONAL GROUPING (174 FEMALE ACoAs)
(3 or more female ACoAs in an occupation: Total of 127 or 73%)

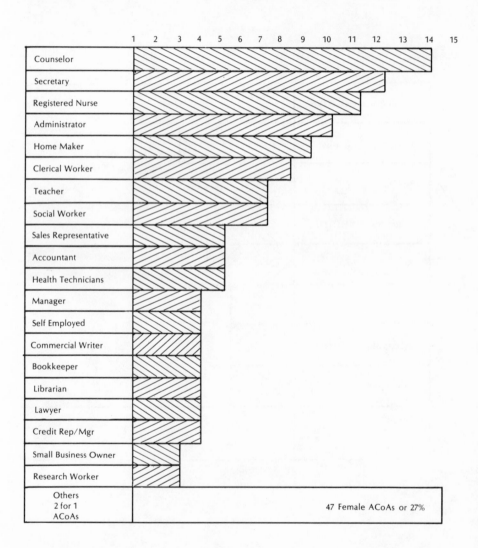

The CoA Teacher

Since I see myself as typical of CoAs who have entered the teaching profession, the best way for me to describe "them" is to let you know "me".

It is only in the past five years or so that I realized the impact of my parents' alcoholism on my life and how I have led that life, including decisions that I have made. Both of my parents are active alcoholics and probably have been for at least the last thirty of my forty-two years.

The only career aspiration I ever had was to be a teacher. I programmed myself to like school before I ever entered. My efforts to do well and to gain recognition paid off in terms of teacher acceptance and personal achievement which continued throughout my academic career. By my own choice I attended Catholic schools from first grade through college . . . sixteen years. I was elected to the National Honor Society, graduated Magna Cum Laude from college and always received exemplary grades in conduct. "Making my parents proud" was my expressed reason for my need to excel, although I was deeply shamed by the occasional lower grade and/or teacher dissatisfaction. I often made deals with God (and with St. Joseph Cupertino, patron saint of test-takers) for inspiration to do well with papers, reports and on tests. It seemed to follow that, having achieved success (well, Elaine did have one-hundredth of a Grade Point Index higher, and therefore was "first" in the class — old patterns die hard!), I was convinced that my decision to be a teacher was a good one.

I liked the sense of control I had in the classroom. I was in charge! I made the rules and, most important, people did what I wanted them to do. A "big fish in a little pond," I believed that my life would have the order and purpose which I was unable to make happen at home with my parents.

And such a teacher! Preparation was accomplished with zeal —not content to have one source, I researched many to leave out nothing. I wonder now if those early lessons made much sense to those 4th graders, chock-full as they were with all of that researched information. This need for being a Super

Teacher points out the other side of that Control Issue: my personal feeling of lack of control accompanied by my fear of exposing the fear and inadequacy I was experiencing.

I strongly saw the need for that classroom to be a place where youngsters felt safe and appreciated — No "what the hell happened with Science, you only got an 'A-' " in my class! I worked very hard to reach every youngster, feeling guilty when I thought about those youngsters who remained shy or ignorant of a subject/chapter/lesson in spite of my hardest efforts to inspire and to educate. Actually, I was angry with them for not coming along. I was frustrated with the lack of success with them. I was hurt that they did not like me. It never occurred to me then that those children might have something in common with me — a dysfunctional, if not alcoholic, family.

When I reached out to those youngsters, equipped with my fear of close relationships and my unfamiliarity with emotional intimacy, I was asking of those children what I was unwilling to give: to share my feelings, fears, worries, my "secrets." I was very sensitive to what I perceived as their rejection.

I also appreciated the isolation of the classroom where I could attempt to be all things to each student without a peer audience. In addition, I prided myself on never asking anyone for help. "I AM CAPABLE" was the facade I held out in front of me for THEM to see; only I knew the scared little girl who held up that Big Front.

To pretend that all was not only well, but excellent, and certainly under control, I decided — the first year that I taught —to have my 4th grade present a play for the other students, and in the evening for parents. (At the time, I was several months pregnant with my first child and determined that none of this would affect the Super Wife I presented to my husband.) Not content to settle for anything "pre-packaged", I wrote the play . . . and the songs (after I had a self-taught crash course in piano-playing) . . . and planned and executed the elaborate scenery (it involved the illusion of descending beneath the ocean and finding an underwater kingdom) . . . and costumes. One day as my class was working on various tasks related to the play (painting, drawing, sewing, singing, rehearsing), the principal entered the room. Walking to a cabinet on her sweep of the room, she came to me and informed me that there was dust on the cabinet. I had managed to find a principal (a woman) with my father's ability to remind me that I would never be ENOUGH. Fascinating how the fear of being found out was tied in with the need to prove myself which led to my over-extension. Incidentally, the play was a great success, but I can only truly appreciate and remember it as such within the recent past.

Ultimately I decided to return to college for a Masters degree in Counseling, again with a dedication to achieving "A's". Reaching that degree, I became a junior high school guidance counselor. I made it a point to understand the master schedule and its planning; I reminded the Director of Guidance of deadlines; I excelled at the efficient expedition of necessary paperwork (which was not the forte of the two men with whom I counseled) so I often did it entirely and usually at home so that my time with students would not be impeded. Throughout all of the above, I was striving to enhance the image of the Guidance Department and to fulfill my prime purpose of being available and helpful to students, and concomitantly to parents and staff. This meant no coffee breaks except at my desk while working. It meant no regular lunch times or departure times. This began to be changed five years ago when I faced up to my problems as the adult child of an alcoholic and began to really live my own life.

The CoA Manager

A manager of the EAP at a high-tech research firm described his observations of CoAs on the job:

The composite profile was that of an individual who was very capable with good credentials, who however lacked self confidence. It is a person who had used the high technology environment to avoid dealing with people. They see themselves as being different, "on the outside looking in", and not really part of the group. They often become so isolated that they can no longer communicate in other than technical terms.

They do not expect anything from relationships beyond technical support and they don't get anything. Their isolation grows until they find themselves in a situation where they can no longer function. All human tasks are reduced to analytical terms, seen through technical paradigms. The smallest social task becomes a major technical issue. Because the interpersonal world is not always logical in technical terms, they feel more and more like a failure using human fallibility as evidence for their lack of self-worth.

By the time these people come to me, they actually do look different in that they often dress in very plain ways, are poorly groomed and seem to have simply dropped out of the social mainstream. These folks are wonderful employees as long as they do not have to interact socially or get involved with "political games". A serious problem is that sometimes they get promoted and make awful supervisors.

As supervisors, they are demanding sometimes unrealistic but don't delegate authority. They do not trust their subordinates and ask to have every assignment repeated over and over. Sometimes, they seem very pleased and the next moment they are screaming at the subordinate in public. Later they may return tearful and apologetic. They can't be pleased.

Some indicate that they feel like a fraud and know that they will be fired if the company finds out what they are really like, even if they are actually very competent. Their victims are their subordinates who come to the EAP feeling abused, terribly confused and often ready to give up.

The CoA Medical Student

Professional schools have always been very stressful places — witness films like *The Paper Chase* about law school — but they are particularly stressful for CoAs. The system is designed to teach humility and confidence, to work to the limits of one's endurance — just what the CoA doctor ordered, as Tom tells us of his experience in medical school:

In the dysfunctional family I grew up in, we were expected to do two things perfectly — schoolwork and being nice to other people. "Perfectly" meant straight 'A's, always having adults compliment your behavior, and doing this all apparently without effort and without mistakes.

I was "perfect" up through college, when I just had to learn, take tests, and no one had to know me. But medical school was different; I went into medical school thinking I'd be a hero who would do something wonderful for people that no one else had ever done. It seems silly, but what else could I do? I'd been taught to get my self-esteem from being better/smarter than everyone else and by making myself liked by everyone.

The first two years were more books and tests — only now there was more work than I could do perfectly. Besides, medical school is full of people who'd been top students, and I was no longer effortlessly best in my class. I got average scores and tried to tell myself I could have been tops if I'd worked at it, but that never satisfied me. No longer being the smartest punctured my self-image.

Medical school is training for novices; and, in truth, we have to learn from our mistakes and from seeing that we need to learn more. But if an attending physician pointed out a mistake I'd made, or something I didn't know (but **should** have), or just didn't seem interested in me, I felt imperfect, bad, and at fault. I didn't want people to see that.

Unfortunately medicine is traditionally taught by taking a top student, giving him more to learn than he can, giving him no priorities as to what to learn — "Everything is important, I wouldn't expect you to learn it if it weren't," and then ridiculing and demeaning him and telling him he's useless until he thinks he got into medical school by mistake.

My perfectionism, people-pleasing, and readiness to accept blame made me an ideal set-up for this system. Throughout most of my medical training, I felt guilty about becoming a doctor. I thought I didn't want it enough to deserve it, that I'd never learn enough to be competent. At the same time I was expected to exude confidence and authority with patients.

The next two years I had to deal with individuals — the doctors who were my teachers (attendings) and my patients. In retrospect, these people were not out to make me miserable, but what I'd learned in my family made these close relationships painful. Growing up I'd been told I was smart and kind. These were the positive attributes I identified with and I *needed to keep hearing them.*

Attendings rarely had time to teach, needed us to do some of their work, and trusted us to do things if only they thought we already knew how. The only way for us to get experience was to pretend we already had it. This didn't fit with my idea of perfect patient care, but I did it, got the experience I needed, and felt guilty and phony.

On the other hand, my patients liked me, listened to me, wanted to see me, and told me I was important to them. I was taught that I should look at patients clinically, but I didn't. I needed some positive strokes. This led to even longer hours as I spent more time with patients. I felt guilty when I went home, because I always felt that there was some patient's need I'd left unattended. I had been taught this as well by attending staff who often sacrificed their personal lives to their patients. And I found myself becoming at ease with the role of caretaker, but not enjoying the rest of my life. Since my personal relationships and free time had never been fun or satisfying, it was easy for me to become a workaholic, even though I started to hate medicine.

The CoA Priest

The workplace is not restricted to the office, the store, or the factory. It can also be the religious community, where the CoA experiences the same problems that occur anywhere else on the job — and then some!

A counselor who deals with religious communities writes:

The ACoA in the religious workplace has all the traits of the typical ACoA, but there are some added complications. Certain elements in the training of priests, religious sisters, and religious brothers seem to be harmful to the ACoA unless they are honestly faced. For instance, religious training frequently has given statements such as these:

"You are called to be a person for others.

You must be all things to all persons.

Service to others is its own reward.

The needs of the community must be addressed before personal needs.

We must strive to be perfect."

The religious ACoA has little or no understanding of the need for personal boundaries within one's ministry. There is a real difference between religious life and the life of a person who has a regular occupation. When you have an occupation, you can try to separate your work life from your personal life. The religious is unable to do this. Thus, it is more difficult to understand the place of boundaries and clearly defined limits in one's work.

The religious ACoA is given strong religious motivation to put others first. Scriptural statements like, "The Son of Man has not come to be served, but to serve, and to give His life as a ransom for many" are frequently applied in ways that are harmful, rather than helpful. ACoAs in general put others first and themselves last, but the religious ACoA is given a powerful theological motivation to do this as well. So when the religious ACoA goes into therapy, there can be tremendous resistance to placing oneself first. It is perceived as not simply a matter of personal well-being. It is seen as a direct contradiction of the religious message that the religious ACoA is supposed to be following.

When the religious ACoA is criticized, there are several different reactions. One reaction is simply the idea that the religious ACoA is a bad person. However, another reaction is directly related to one's religious calling. If you are criticized for what you do in your ministry, you are not only letting down another person, you are letting down God. Thus, rather than realizing that we often can and do make mistakes, the whole foundation of one's religious commitment is indeed questioned.

Statements like this come into the mind of the religious ACoA: "If I have done this, then I must not be a good priest. I am a fraud in my religious vocation. I help no one. People can see through me."

ACoAs can feel that they are frauds as people. The religious ACoAs believe that they are frauds as people and as the type of person that they believe God has called them to be.

Loneliness is a particularly acute phenomenon for the reli-

*gious ACoA. While the idea of living within a religious com-
munity theoretically means that sharing can take place, this is
often the last place where the religious ACoA can share. When
others appear to be striving for perfection, the religious ACoA
may feel that he or she is really trying to admit their imperfec-
tion. This builds up the isolation and creates yet another com-
plication for the religious ACoA.*

*Intimacy and sexuality are different issues for the religious
ACoA who is celibate. The religious reason for celibacy is that
one is able to be loving and open with all and can truly serve all
in the community. The negative side of this for the religious
ACoA is that they truly need to share their deepest feelings and
thoughts. They need to share their past experiences and admit
their present inadequacies. But sometimes the religious life
may not foster this type of experience, so the sense of loneliness and isolation increases; the ability to be intimate and loving decreases. Obviously, persons who are married or in relationships frequently are unable to be intimate and loving. But
it seems that the nature of religious life provides a greater
sense of loneliness and isolation than other vocations.*

The CoA Foreman

As children, we were often told, "Work very hard and you'll
be rewarded." Companies sometimes support and reinforce
this message. Hank is a case in point — a guy who worked so
hard that he almost lost his job!

*I've worked for a public utility for about 14 years now, and of
those 14 years, approximately 12 of them were spent at a power
plant. I began with the company as a laborer, worked very
hard, long hours outside in the the field, since then I went
"inside" to the power plant.*

*I was always taught that if you work very hard, you'll be
rewarded by a job, so to speak, or a promotion. I've now found
out that it's a little different. When I went into the power plant,
I began as a Stockman. What I did in this position was off-load
trucks, along with various paper work, until I moved up into
my position as a Material Clerk, which consisted of controlling
40,000 or so spare parts.*

My job was to see that each part was classified and broken down into sub-systems and defined as either mechanical, electrical or instrumentation parts, and then to assign each a particular six-digit catalogue number, which referenced that part to the part number and established a minimum/maximum for the part, and then find it and store it in one of eight warehouses. Also there was a ledger system and an index so that when the various personnel came in, they would be able to locate the part they wanted. This manual system was also transferred into a computer. I worked very hard and very long (ten hours per day, seven days a week). In fact, I averaged 550 to 575 hours of overtime per year. My travel time to and from work was an hour's drive, so I would get up at 5:30 each morning to go to work and would leave work to come home around 5:45 p.m.

This still wasn't enough work for me because I spent four-and-a-half years building a house, and I would sometimes stay up until 3:00 a.m., sleep on my way to work (because I car pooled), sleep on my lunch hours, catch another couple of hours sleep after work, then get up around 9:00 p.m. and work most of the night on the house. I was always taught that if you want something, you have to work for it.

I went through a marriage, and I just came out of a relationship, and I found out at age 35, which I am now, that I really don't know who the hell I am! Everybody looks at me and idolizes me because I can do everything.

Like I said, I built that house — framed it, did all the plumbing, the electrical work, designed it, insulated it, dry-walled it, spackled it, sanded it, wallpapered it, did the outside stone work (with the help of some friends), etc. The house is approximately 3,500 sq. ft., and it has 13 rooms, and I'm the only one living there! This sounds funny, but it's true. I found out that my life-long dream was actually more like my coffin.

On my job I would never refuse overtime. In fact, nine of those eleven-and-a-half years on my company rating report, I was described as a very loyal employee, never refusing overtime and always being willing and available for work. I thought that was good. You work for a company, you're a responsible individual. It was part of your job assignment to do that when something happened in this particular operation, which ran 24 hours a day, seven days a week, holidays included. I worked many Easters, Thanksgivings and double shifts. I would go home, be called back out, and off I'd go again. I had it good there. It paid well, and I had many good benefits. I had a stove at work, a crockpot, a blender, but I found out that when my job was done (eleven other people left that job because it was "crazy" or "not worth it"), I was the only one who had stuck it out because I had confidence in my ability.

But this got me into a lot of trouble. It caused my divorce, because I would never say "no" to overtime or work. I got into many arguments with my immediate supervisor because I carried things too far at times in trying to be a perfectionist.

I would always be too serious. People always tell me I'm too serious — I never laughed. It got to the point where I wouldn't even socialize with my friends because I felt my job was more important, and I wanted to get ahead, so I worked very hard for this. In fact, I even went to school for three years to get a Purchasing Degree. I joined the Purchasing Management Association (none of the company buyers, other than the Head Buyer, belonged to this association), and this cost me money for which I wasn't even reimbursed, and I even took personal vacation to attend a seminar so I could get one point towards my certification at the university.

I felt this was good. I was gearing myself towards a better position. I made it my point that when I attended a meeting of the PMA every week, I would take my own time and have lunch with one of the buyers and discuss work. When the job was done, though, the system was functioning, and I was bored!

By being bored, I got into trouble. I was picked to join the Activities Committee, the Safety and Health Committee, Plant Betterment Committee, Fire Protection Committee, and I belonged to all of these! I started running company bus trips, which got to be once a month, then once every weekend, and then twice and even three times every weekend. People were calling me at work constantly, and this caused problems with my immediate supervisor and his supervisor. They thought I wasn't "doing my job" because they considered this a sideline, even though it was company-oriented. I was told I would only be given an hour per week for doing these activities. But I kept on doing it until I got reprimanded and was told either to stop or be removed from the committee. I was VP of the Committee at the time for approx. one thousand people. When I took over the position, the "kitty" was almost in the red, but at the end of the year we were $1,000.00 in the black.

So I thought I was doing a good job in that respect. I was neglecting my duties on my full-time job, but the job was done and everything was running smoothly. Even so, this was a problem for the company because I didn't seem to be there, and my supervisor got very upset over having to answer my phone all the time. I finally decided to take a voluntary demotion, and I left that installation to be closer to Corporate Headquarters.

My voluntary demotion was a mistake. I lost $153.00 a week and went from a B-8 status down to a B-2 just so I could be closer to the Corporate office, figuring they would recognize that I have all this experience under my belt, my certifications, membership in the PMA, etc. I had bid on several jobs and was turned down for various reasons. My former boss of nine years retired, and I put in for his position. I didn't hear for approximately two months, and then I got a letter in the mail. I didn't even open it up because I was so confident in getting an interview for the position. I had even gone out and bought a new suit, new shoes, etc. for my big interview. Well, lo and behold, when I opened the letter I found that, out of 30 other applicants, I was placed on a level where I wouldn't even be considered for an interview.

This was the reason I went to see the counselor, and she said that I looked like somebody had taken a knife and cut me in half. I felt, boy oh boy, I had put all my eggs in one basket, and look what happened!

Of course, I was told not to be discouraged because something will eventually come my way, and I believe it will. The day I got that rejection letter, I walked and walked and walked for at least five miles on my lunch hour, and I wasn't even going to return to work. I was going to say "BS" to the company, but the bottom line is that the company really doesn't owe me anything other than 40 hours pay for 40 hours work, but I guess that I'm obsessed with being a perfectionist and in thinking that if you work hard for a company, you go down with the company like the captain of a sinking ship.

The CoA Airline Employee

Another EAP counselor, working this time in the airline industry, says this about his CoA workers:

ACoAs who come to me for help often have a very strong work history and are often self and supervisor described as very conscientious. For those whose job performance was deficit and referred by supervision, I noticed that I was able to trace a historical point when excellent performance was interrupted by a progressive decline. CoAs often report that their performance on the job and the company are very important to them.

The advent of deregulation has resulted in a change from a nurturing paternalistic management style to one that is demanding and results oriented and a more pressured work environment. Some ACoAs adjust well to these changes and appear to identify with the needed company changes as a survival need. Some experience an anxiety and pain related to being unable to please passengers or respond to their demands or not being affirmed by supervisors as in the past.

ACoAs appear more likely to assume a special care-taking relationship with troubled employees (co-dependents). This is reflected in supervisors and co-workers who invest energy in helping and taking responsibility for the maintenance of their jobs. They have often sought help in the past that did not address their needs.

It appears that many of their problems are related to interpersonal difficulties that often escalate and cause a great deal of anxiety. This is often connected with family difficulties that have become unmanageable. Often the loss and abandonment themes seem to be connected with this issue, and result in either job deterioration or a great deal of energy expended on the job to no effect.

The CoA Administrator

Bureaucracy often provides the firm guidelines children of alcoholics need to have — where they stand in relation to their fellow employees, what they are supposed to do — but these boundaries can often mean nothing to a hardworking CoA. They also have the ability to turn a part-time job into a full-time occupation, as Bill shows here in his account of the work he did to support his graduate studies.

I was involved in the dormitory administration of a big university on the west coast, first as a Front Desk staffer, later as a Front Desk Supervisor, and finally as an acting Front Desk Manager. I achieved this in the space of only three years, during which I also worked full-time on my graduate studies, participated in residence halls' politics, and worked on behalf of the students in my department on the Graduate Fine Arts Council. Somewhere in there, I was also trying to conduct a "meaningful" relationship with a fellow student.

From the start, I was very hard-working and conscientious. In part, it was out of gratitude for having a job where I lived — just a hallway away. And it had come at a time when I was still waiting for my student loan and had no money at all, so I also felt indebted to the people who hired me. I worked all kinds of shifts — daytime and late-night. I did all kinds of special jobs and projects that demanded a great deal of attention to detail. And I know that I did it well. I was pleasant to work with, was pleasant to the hall residents and the rest of the staff. I was popular and eager to solve problems.

After being on the staff for a year and a half, working both the Christmas and summer breaks, I was offered the supervisor position. Despite the fact that I was in the middle of preparing for my comprehensive exams, I took on the job.

From the start as supervisor, I began to do more and more at the Front Desk. It wasn't just a matter of the added responsibilities of the job; it was a matter of picking up on **everything** *that was happening there. Nothing could happen without my supervision, without my approval. I was on call 24 hours a day, and I had a real sense of anxiety every time I left the building. One time, I jokingly told a friend that as the dorm sank into the sea,*

I would be standing at the salute on the bridge. Some joke.

I began to feel that I was overextending myself, so I dropped the residence hall and campus politics over the summer. But then I had too much time on my hands — too much for the Front Desk, although I was working about thirty hours a week; too much for my papers and academic work, although that was taking up another forty or fifty; too much for trying to make the relationship work. As a result, I took on a research assistantship to fill in the quiet hours.

I took tremendous care of my staff as supervisor. Since I was taking several independent study courses, I spent less time in the classroom. So when one of the staff had an exam to prepare for, I would take over their shift. When a resident was having a problem with a roommate, I would talk with them both about it and help them try to solve it.

The one thing I did not play by the book when I was supervisor was the huge amount of paperwork. It was my conviction that the purpose of bureaucracy of that sort was to lay blame, and I wanted my staff to know and feel that I had trust and confidence in them, even though I was spending so much time down at the Front Desk that trust wasn't really an issue — I would always be there for them, quite literally.

The manager retired after I had finally passed my exams, and since I knew the job so well, I thought I was the logical successor. But the university was in the midst of a hiring freeze, and all I could do was assume the role of the manager but not the title or the pay. I felt, in a sense, that I had to take on the added responsibilities because the general manager of the dorm was new to the job and didn't know how it worked. And I was told, in any case, that a special exemption might be made for our dorm and that I would get the position very soon.

The "soon" was first two months, then three. I spoke vaguely to my boss about my getting some kind of pay raise, but pay scales had been frozen in the freeze, too. I asked him about filing for the exemption and he said that he "would look into it". I began to get a little restless as three months dragged into six.

Then I decided to take action. I wrote the University

Ombudsman, the Residence Halls Administrator, and the Dean responsible for university housing. I said nothing about any of this to my boss, but I found that I was getting tired of working at the Front Desk, tired of the hassles with the girlfriend, and generally tired of the university. I started to smoke a lot of dope and work on my music. I took no classes at all in my final term and worked at the desk only during the days. I was waiting for something — anything — to happen.

And things did happen, in quick succession. The first thing that happened was that the Ombudsman's office had called my boss, not me, and I was brought into his office.

"How could you do this to me?"

I responded that I felt I had no choice, that he wasn't doing anything for me.

He replied that he had assumed responsibility for the work I was doing and that I was making him look bad. I apologized, then turned around and fired off a memo to the Residence Halls Administrator saying that I was still doing all of this work and enclosed the job descriptions of the Front Desk Supervisor and the Front Desk Manager.

Nothing more happened after that, although I did have another unproductive meeting with my boss. A week later, my girlfriend, supposedly in the middle of summer classes, asked me to put something in her room during the day. I went in that morning and found her in bed with someone else. I couldn't believe it, and even now I wonder if it wasn't some kind of hallucination. Whatever the case, I immediately went down to the desk and wrote up my resignation. I finally had the excuse I needed to get away.

The CoA Nurse

Children of alcoholics very often find themselves in human service occupations, as this nursing supervisor describes:

Nurses are very proud of the fact that they are caretakers; they tend to the suffering and deal with death on a regular basis. It feels good to assist in relieving another's pain. With this in mind, the sense of responsibility that a CoA nurse will carry in the name of her patients is overwhelming. She may even *shoulder this responsibility to the point of believing she can hold back death itself.*

The small successes and experience of another's joy in the painstaking process of recovery encourage the CoA nurse to want more. These experiences, combined with the expectations that others have of her, compel the CoA nurse to demand more of herself. She will think nothing of trying to fulfill the following roles: counselor, healer, wife, mother, technician, manager, transporter and M.D. assistant. Denial is evident, for the CoA nurse is far removed from the impossibility of what she expects of herself.

Guilt is a wonderful motivator for nurses who are viewed by the public as "angels of mercy" and "self-sacrificing" people. Saying "no" is just not an acceptable way for a nurse to deal with her limitations. Consequently, nurses become skilled manipulators, "deal makers", and controllers of their environment. If these methods don't work, tempers flare up, "martyrdom", and "excuse-making" will.

Generally, a CoA nurse will readily give up her own instincts and thoughts about her work, a patient or situation in the presence of an M.D. This surrender by the nurse occurs less frequently with supervisors, but nonetheless it does happen. These people are intimidating to the CoA, for they represent authority. They are all-knowing and have power.

Among her peers, the CoA nurse occasionally releases her emotions — most often in the form of anger. Wittiness and humor work well to relieve the nurse's load. Resentment, self-pity and resignation weigh her down. When asked about her feelings, the CoA nurse quickly deflects the question, gives excuses or flatly denies their existence. Clearly she is uncomfortable, quite possibly because she is out of touch with her feelings.

The thought of changing her situation or expanding her abilities are met with an air of sadness. Once again the CoA offers excuses or simply resigns herself to her plight.

It is not a surprise that the CoA nurse takes pride in creating calm out of chaotic situations. She is a true artist, a magician in seeming to perform the impossible. She returns each day to meet her challenge, for she knows it well, it is a place that feels like home.

The CoA Waitress

Ever see a waitress carry five plates — four on one arm and a plate in the other hand — take orders on the way to the table for two cups of coffee and a glass of water and still give the right food to the right customer, all from memory? That may be enough for most people to handle, but with a CoA on the job, there's always something more to be done!

When I was 13, I worked as a waitress for a man who owned a pizzeria. Much of the time we were in the restaurant alone. His business was a bomb, from the food to the wallpaper; he was a very unhappy man. I wanted to make his business an overnight success and solve all his personal problems. I shared my ideas with him and began to make arrangements to help him remodel. I thought that I could help his business flourish, then his personal problems would be solved too. I cared so much that he tried to bang me in the kitchen. My mother found out about this through a careless slip of my tongue and promptly called him on it scaring the man to tears. He called me, crying and apologizing. Had my mother not intervened, I would've gone back to work although I was scared out of my mind. Confronting my boss was more terrifying to me than going back.

When I was 16, I worked in a "fine dining" restaurant that was also a bomb. I remained there loyally for about eight months, although I was being exploited in several ways. At times I did the work of a manager and cashier at a waitress's wages ($1.35/hr.) just to "keep busy." My employer once charged me over $100.00 for cashiering mistakes on credit cards, in spite of the fact that it wasn't my job to handle money and that no one had ever trained me. Naturally, I paid him and reprimanded myself for making the mistakes. My employment there ended after a few such incidents, when the Board of Labor and Department of Health became involved.

Most of my restaurant jobs have had similarly dramatic endings. I tend to get so emotionally involved in my work that there is no separation between my job and personal life. In the beginning my employers like me because I compulsively overwork. Then I begin to get resentful and emotional because no one is considering my feelings and I usually get fired shortly thereafter.

Presently I waitress at a restaurant that is very poorly managed. When I first started working there, I worked much harder than humanly possible. If I was the only waitress on and the dining room was jammed, I panicked at how I was going to take care of all 1,000,000 customers. The thought never entered my mind that maybe they should hire an additional waitress.

The CoA Athlete

Nobody knows better than a CoA how to turn play into work. Because they have difficulty in simply having fun, the games others enjoy in childhood become much more serious. Mark's story is typical of CoAs who have made a career of something that others do for fun, whether it's in sports or music. While other people dream of having a career they can enjoy, a CoA, in following such a career, puts a lot of effort into making sure he gets no joy out of it at all.

The ACoA Super Achiever Athlete (ACoA-SAA) will sacrifice many childhood activities in order to excel in athletics. He may pass up playing with his friends in order to spend time practicing. He may also give up soft drinks, sweets and more, in order to perfect his body.

The ACoA-SAA goes to school to compete and succeed in sports and bring worth to his family and self. College and pro scouts don't recruit players from the local Boys Club or YMCA, so school is an important institution in which to participate. He studies enough to maintain his 2.5 GPA and continue competing for the school (If his grades are higher, it is an added bonus).

Like other children of alcoholics, he also spends a great amount of time daydreaming. He will be daydreaming about the winning basket, touchdown, or home run, just as his teacher asks him a question. It is important to him to try to see himself as a winner because he has to battle constantly with an inner voice that tells him he is worthless, unlovable, and a failure.

The ACoA-SAA is loyal to his school and coaches. No one wears the school colors louder or prouder. He brings prestige to the school via the media and community acknowledgment. He is usually the team captain and demands the respect of his peers. He sometimes thinks of himself as a player/coach. He will push himself and his teammates to their physical limitations in order to prepare for competition.

Some people may say, "It's not whether you win or lose, but how you play the game," but this is blasphemy to the ACoA-SAA. He lives for game nights. He lives to "win, win, win", because games are his only opportunity to gain recognition and self-respect. If his team wins, he cannot sleep that night because he cannot stop wondering what good things the newspaper will say the following morning. His sense of self-worth depends solely on the printed article and reported statistics.

But the ACoA-SAA is not an impenetrable fortress in the heat of competition; he is actually the most likely to crack under the stress of a game because of the inner voice of failure. There is nothing more awful for him than to hear the 'voice' while attempting to shoot the winning free throw, toss the winning pitch, catch the winning pass, or sprint the winning lap. The 'voice' appears inconsistently, but always in the key moment of the competition. When he hears it, his concentration breaks and he makes crucial mistakes.

He interprets losing a game as his individual responsibility and not the team's. The inner voice of failure echoes loudly throughout his mind, "You are a failure. You blew it again!" He has brief suicidal thoughts. He thinks there is nothing to live for since he has failed everyone who depends on him. He might put his thoughts into action because his self-worth, which was strictly rooted in athletic success, has been shattered. However, he will not display his depression outwardly because he must maintain his stable public image to please others.

He does not compete well at home in front of everyone he knows because he is trying too hard to please the crowd and is rarely relaxed. If he goes away to college and returns to compete against a local school, he will not play well; the inner voice is too loud.

Because he is a people-pleaser, he will allow his peers at school to control his life in the hallways and classrooms. He would rather be alone, though, because he knows he is really a loser.

The ACoA-SAA is most prone to injuries during stressful periods of the season. Consciously, he prepares himself to be in the best physical shape possible for the season, especially for the very important games. Subconsciously, his mind (if under a great deal of internal/external stress) may cause his body to be susceptible to injury. The injury will occur prior to or in the middle of the competition. It will give him a safe excuse not to face the inner voice of failure. Therefore, he won't have to take the chance of losing and blaming himself once again. No one else could possibly blame him for the team's loss if he was physically incapable of competing.

The ACoA-SAA's choice of which college to attend is also affected by the inner voice of failure. Though he has the ability to compete at a large university, he will more likely select a smaller school. It is much safer to be a big fish in a small pond. However, this does not guarantee success at the collegiate level. Only if he can continue to fight the 'voice', and if he gets enough exposure, he might make it to the professional level of competition.

The 'voice' follows the ACoA-SAA into the professional level, bringing the same emotional havoc he's always known. The inner voice will affect his contract negotiations, his ability to compete, and his emotional stability. This is when he is most likely to use alcohol and drugs on a steady basis.

The CoA in the Military

Not all jobs present the CoA with boundary problems. Sometimes, as Alan says in his description of military life, they can provide the CoA with all the rules he needs to get by:

As an Adult Child of an Alcoholic where better could I find approval and affirmation than in the military. I received instant and lasting recognition from my accomplishments. I spent 20 years in the Navy, the first 12 as a practicing alcoholic, the remainder in recovery. The military offered the perfect atmosphere for this rule-bound ACoA. The system encourages workaholism, unquestioning loyalty, super-responsibility, and no question or doubt of superiors. The system is rigid and demanding. It dictates what normal is . . . I was home.

My uniform set me apart and I instantly achieved status. I wore many of my accomplishments on my chest — awards and ribbons ranging from combat action and achievement to foreign decorations. My gold wings further enhanced my position. On my collar and sleeve you could see my status in the hierarchy and my length of service. In the Navy after 12 years of good conduct (what else?) the red service stripes are replaced with gold ones.

In my personnel record you can find numerous letters of commendation, achievement and appreciation. Also in this file are my semi-annual performance ratings. They are excellent. Of course I wrote my own evaluations for six years. My record also contained six job speciality codes and 35 correspondence courses I had completed.

I loved crisis and there was a lot of it in Military Medicine. My 20 years as a Hospital Corpsman was a rush! I worked in emergency rooms, drove ambulances, and flew helicopters doing search and rescue work — this in addition to managing clinics and supervising others. My approach to management was to give 150%, and, "I'll do it so the job is done right". I was rewarded for my workaholism with more tasks being assigned to me.

Other ACoAs I knew behaved in much the same manner as I. There was a pilot who flew three combat sorties per day when he could have flown two, the acceptable standard. There were many who survived on three hours of sleep or less for days on end in order to meet the "can do" edict of the command.

In my drinkings years I looked for a boss who had a drinking problem or another ACoA. I was enabled for years by both. There were many chances to confront me, yet what problem drinker or ACoA would or could violate the "no talk" rule?

During my last year in the service I experienced abandonment. I was transferred from the Navy to the Marines. I had spent 19 years being a "good sailor" and I felt devastated by this turn of events.

It was also at this time that I first discovered an article concerning Adult Children of Alcoholics. It talked about issues that I had been living with but had not recognized. Once I began to understand them, I could deal with all the other issues in my life. This made my transition from the military to civilian life much easier, since I could understand the feelings I was encountering.

Chapter 2

THE HOME
AWAY FROM HOME

Regardless of the nature of the work or the status of the occupation, CoAs have similar feelings about themselves on the job and about their work.

The following charts indicate the overwhelming degree to which CoAs feel inadequate. There is no indication that these feelings have a basis in the rational world.

Feelings of inadequacy, being unappreciated, boredom, and perfectionism create stress. The stress is created primarily from using energy to repress these feelings and from keeping others from discovering them. The stress is further exasperated because of the lack of understanding of how to address these feelings in constructive ways.

As a result, historic issues get played out in the workplace just as they do everywhere else. It is not suprising then to find that it is not unusual for the CoA to find that his workplace home is not at all unlike his childhood home.

──────────── **FIGURE 2.0** ────────────

TOTAL ACoA FEELINGS GROUPING (236)*
(Feelings Expressed by 3 or more ACoAs: 206 ACoAs or 87%)

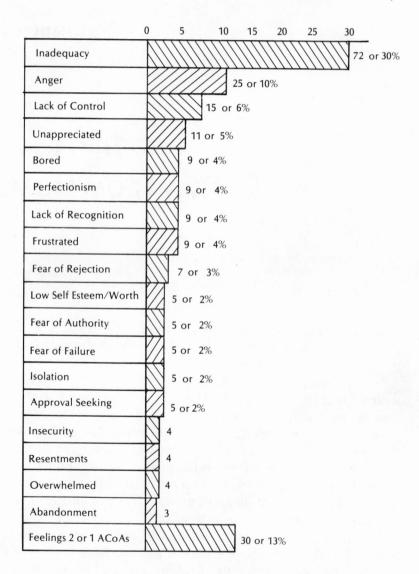

─────────── FIGURE 2.1 ───────────

MALE ACoA FEELINGS GROUPING (64)*
(Feelings Expressed by 3 or more male ACoAs: 41 Male ACoAs or 64%)

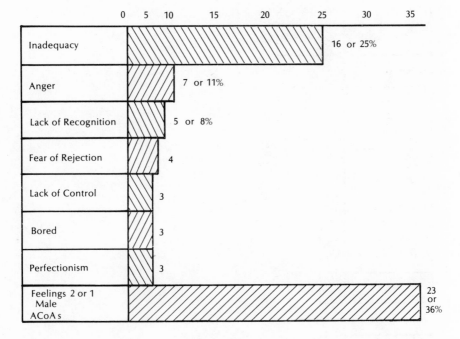

FIGURE 2.2

FEMALE ACoA FEELINGS GROUPING (172)*
(Feelings expressed by 3 or more female ACoAs: 146 females or 85%)

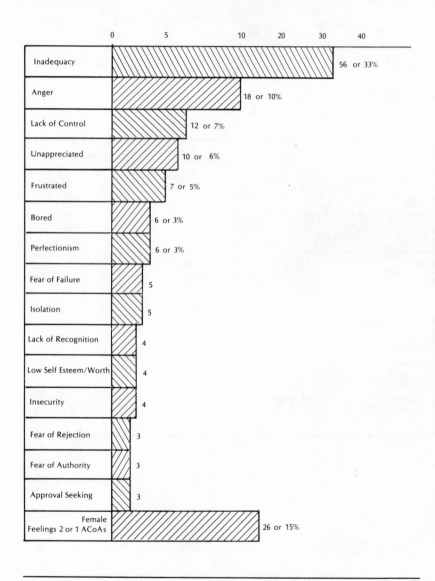

Duplicating the Family of Origin

In many ways the workplace is a home away from home. Co-workers become siblings and those in authority take on the role of parent. That is just the way it is.

Where the workplace differs from the home is the degree of intimacy one experiences there. Since CoAs have difficulty with boundaries, it is very hard for them to maintain an appropriate and comfortable social and emotional climate with their supervisors and peers. The relationships are unclear as the CoAs swing between trying to "parent" their superiors and being enabled by their peers.

As a result, unresolved anger and dependency needs will be played out in their work relationships.

This is only one aspect of the co-dependency. Another aspect that surfaces is covering up for those who exhibit alcohol and drug problems. They also enable by picking up the slack for those who don't do their part. This is encouraged by the system. "We all pitched in" is a fairly common idea that management likes to foster among their employees.

Once the co-dependency begins, conditions invariably worsen regardless of the job situation and the CoA will either take on total responsibility or give it all away. The reality is that once the co-dependency takes over, reason leaves and is replaced by fantasy. This happens very slowly and so is most difficult to realize in the moment. Eventually anger and fear alternate as the prevailing responses to the work environment occur, with the occasional plateau where the CoA believes that everything is fine — until the next time. It is a repeat of childhood.

I include an example of this process by someone I know well. She is a very capable conscientious professional who is very much aware of her co-dependent responses. I mention that so you can keep in mind that the awareness is only the first step — without it, growth is impossible. But awareness without action is of dubious value.

I am an ACoA and an Alcoholism Counselor. I am one of ten children. My mother is the alcoholic. She is a periodic binge drinker, the standard Jekyll-and-Hyde alcoholic. When sober, she is beautiful, brilliant, caring and responsible. When drinking, she is ugly, sick and unavailable for a week or two weeks at a time. Father is a text book co-alcoholic. He is himself the son of two alcoholic parents. He abstains from alcohol. He is a self-made man, the breadwinner of the family, the one who takes over as much as possible when mother is drinking. My brothers and sisters all have at least one of the identified roles adopted by alcoholic children. Growing up I assumed the roles of mascot, lost child and family hero.

I am 27 years old, three years recovering from my own alcohol and drug dependency, two years in ACoA and Al-Anon, and a year and a half in therapy with a wonderful, very skillful therapist. Severe depression, anxiety and a problematic marriage brought me to therapy. The process of therapy for me was hard and painful. As I moved through the muck, the depression lifted and I gained a perspective on where I came from, how it affected me and what I need to be doing in the present. I began to not feel guilty about taking care of myself. This new perspective changed my behavior, my thinking and my feelings. I finished the necessary course work for certification and my master's degree program. I separated from my husband, then I had no job and no money. I kept going to meetings, therapy and I got a job.

The agency where I work is an out-patient treatment center. The clientele are primarily alcoholic and chemically dependent. The staff is basically trained in chemical dependency. The organizational structure is an executive director, three program supervisors, four full-time therapists and four part-time therapists. The similarities between being one of a staff of twelve and being one from a family of twelve never crossed my mind. I was hired at the same time as two other full-time therapists. Our primary supervisor is Bob. Bob is attractive, witty and well versed in therapeutic interventions. During the first three months of this job, I divorced my husband and developed very intimate relationships with my co-workers. The work schedule was extremely difficult. I worked primarily in the evenings and I was expected to carry 25 individual clients, as well as families and groups in a 40-hour work-week. It is a community agency, so no one is turned away.

I was feeling good about myself as an individual as well as with what I was doing with my clients and co-workers. During this period, I was not alone in wondering what was happening in my life. The other therapists were also working to get acclimatized and settled.

Relatively early on, I started asking questions, sometimes getting answers to my questions, sometimes not. My supervisor would tell me he would get back to me and would forget, or not attend to the question asked.

The staff brought new skills, new ambitions and new energy into this agency. We presented our ideas, thoughts and feelings on new programs, new groups, and new treatment to the supervisor and to the administrator. They'd agree, they'd acknowledge that all of these ideas and programs were needed and necessary. They encouraged us to go on.

When we asked for what we needed to carry out this work, they would tell us that they would get back to us and didn't. The months continued and the frustration grew. We began to notice that the supervisors would play ball with responsibility. They would toss responsibility from one to the other, back to the administrator, back down to the supervisors and come back to the staff with nothing — no concrete answers to the questions, no materials or support for the therapists to do their jobs. When I got in touch with my frustration, I initially would try to use one of my three programs by reminding myself during these moments to "Let go and let God." I found out that I could no longer "let go and let God" when there wasn't a chair for the client or somebody to answer the phones that were constantly ringing.

All of the line staff identified feelings of abandonment, anger and frustration. As a group we supported each other and helped each other to get through the moment. As individuals we would go back to the supervisor and ask again for what we needed. Sixty percent of the time we didn't get what we needed, 20 percent of the time he wouldn't be there to ask, and 20 percent of the time we got what we needed.

I tried to respect the supervisor and his authority, until I realized that he was not worthy of my respect. The staff then consulted with the administrator on the problems we had in dealing with the supervisor. She would console us and tell us it was wrong and that she would do something about it.

She would then meet individually with the supervisor and let him know that she expected a change. There would be a brief period of change with the supervisor relapsing back to his old behavior, irresponsible and unpredictable.

As this pattern continued, the frustration became familiar. I knew it was from somewhere else as well. At a staff meeting one day I sat at the end of the table and looked at the faces. I looked at the administrator and I looked at the supervisors. There were twelve people there, I could identify that what I was reacting to was my family of origin. My supervisor and his behavior was my alcoholic mother. The administrator who consoled and worked hard and wished that things would change was my father. Several of the other staff, the quiet ones, were the lost children. There were also mascots and family heroes on the staff.

I had developed a new role here that I never had in my own family. I was a scapegoat. The supervisors felt that I was stirring up the trouble. If it wasn't for my complaints and my demands, everyone would feel better on the job. There were statements being made during the staff meeting but I couldn't hear them. I continuously looked around the table. I identified which of these staff people were my 'brothers' or 'sisters'. I clearly saw what I was reacting to and it made me more angry. I was enraged that a treatment facility working with sick individuals and families could let this happen.

When I gained this insight along with my anger, I experienced hope, hope that now that I knew what it was that was going on, now that the problem was identified, that changes could be made.

I met with the administrator and shared my thoughts with her. Ironically she is the ex-wife of an alcoholic. I told her that I thought she was enabling the supervisor by allowing him to continue his destructive behavior patterns. Again, I let her *know that his behavior was affecting me and other staff members.*

She would then turn to another supervisor who was more responsible to have him clean up the mess. That would work for a week. My resentment continued to grow.

The administrator created problems because she didn't want to hurt anyone. Her answer to the problem of Bob was to change his position from supervisor to public relations.

In the remaining time I never saw Bob do his job as a public relations person either. I was relieved with this insight. I could see so clearly what I was reacting to. Once I saw that there would be no change, I felt empowered. I had to leave to take care of myself. This I did. I had left home once and I could do it again. At least this time I recognized my powerlessness and having done my best, knew I had to move on.

Another example of an alcoholic family system involved Jean. Jean is a keypunch operator and has been for 20 years. Her company is installing a new machine and she is terrified that she will be unable to learn the system and will lose her job. She gets paralyzed at the training sessions.

The person in charge of the training explains things quickly, and leaves out important information. Those who know her say she does this because she is frightened that if others get too good, she will lose her authority.

When someone asks a question, she makes the person wait for the answer while she does makeshift work. The trainee is sitting in the office doing nothing while everyone else is busy. The trainee feels awkward and awful, and becomes certain they are all aware of the fact she is stupid. When the question is finally answered, it's answered in such a way as to imply that anyone with half a brain would have understood it the first time.

A typical response to this behavior would be anger, not paralysis. It therefore becomes important to discover what the paralysis means.

In growing up, Jean was always told by her alcoholic father how stupid she was and she believed him. She was also told to do things around the house but never told how and then got yelled at if she asked. She would then get beaten if she didn't do it right. She knew it had to do with her because she didn't think the same thing happened to her twin sister. She found out later that it did happen to her sister, but her sister suffered more silently.

It, therefore, is no surprise that Jean would become frozen when placed in a situation which is so much like her childhood. It is a replay of the same system.

The difference here is that with this insight, Jean no longer has to be the victim and can take action to ensure that she will be treated in a more respectful manner.

Co-dependency in its simplest terms is a loss of personal power. It is characterized by giving over control of one's ego to another.

If co-dependency is loosely defined as the giving away of personal power, the answers lie in how to be personally powerful and maintain it; how to be active and not reactive; how to take appropriate responsibility but not allow others to induce guilt.

In the first case the answer lay in leaving the job, in the second case, the answer lay in being more confrontive.

Functioning within the first system became impossible. In the second one, when the training is complete, the contact with the person who precipitates the co-dependent response is also over.

The context in which the bad feelings emerge is relevant to the resolution.

Chapter Three

CoAs as Employees

Much of the inner struggle that the CoA faces in the work place results from childhood myths. The myths had an effect on how one behaved and felt in the classroom during childhood and in adult life play themselves out in the work environment.

Myths are a part of a belief system. They substantiate our sense of who we are. The beliefs are internalized and are held onto both consciously and unconsciously. They are the result of childhood messages, and unless challenged, they are believed well into adult life. Once these myths are challenged, there is a sense of disbelief for CoAs, followed by relief that the baggage no longer has to be carried. But giving them up is not automatic. It requires hard work. Some popularly held myths include:

IF I DON'T GET ALONG WITH MY BOSS, IT IS MY FAULT.

There is something wrong with me if I cannot make this relationship go right. There is something wrong with me if my boss doesn't treat me the way I ought to be treated. There is something wrong with me if I cannot relate to my boss.

Then again, maybe it doesn't mean there is something wrong

with you. Maybe there is simply something wrong, or maybe there is something wrong with your boss.

The important question is, "Why, if you cannot relate to your boss and you have tried in all the ways that you know how, do you stay?" What keeps you stuck? Why not consider working someplace else? The decision to leave a bad situation does not automatically mean that you have failed. Recognizing the breakdown of your working relationship may mean that you are beginning to take better care of yourself.

There are many reasons why work situations are undesirable. You may not get along with your boss and it may not have anything to do with a deficiency in either of you. It may come from philosophic differences that you both are unwilling to compromise. Seeking out organizations that are more in line with your thought may make for a healthier work environment for you.

It may also be that your supervisor reminds you too closely of that alcoholic parent whose approval you sought and could never achieve. You judge yourself because you "should be able to handle it better now that you are in recovery". Why should you have to handle it? Why should you use all that energy to remain stable when you could be using it in ways that will enhance your growth? Leaving a work situation that is unhealthy for you is **not** the same as the "geographic cure" taken by alcoholics.

IF I AM NOT PRODUCTIVE, I AM WORTHLESS.

The worth of a person has nothing to do with productivity. You are worthy simply because you are. This is contrary to your early conditioning, so trying to prove your worth is automatic to you. A man I know as a result of therapy divested himself of one aspect of his professional responsibilities. It took three people to replace him. He told me that as a child he learned that he simply could not trust his parents to be there for him. Not only did he have to take care of himself but they continued to put him down. They told him that he was no good, he was worthless, he was stupid, he was incompetent. He believed them, but he couldn't trust them to help him find ways out of his struggle. So he relied on himself because he couldn't rely on anybody else. Although he couldn't believe in them, he believed their message. As a result, he didn't feel good about himself but continued to have to prove he was OK to himself because he couldn't trust anybody else to do it.

IF I'M NOT SUITED FOR THE JOB I'M SUPPOSED TO BE SUITED FOR, THERE IS SOMETHING WRONG WITH ME.

Other people have said to you you'd be an ideal teacher or you really should be an adminstrator or you really should take this promotion. But something within you says that's not where you want to be, that it doesn't feel right to you. Still, you believe that the only reason it doesn't feel right is because there's something wrong with you. You've known for so long that other people know what's best for you, that what's going to feel good exists outside of you, and if something inside tells you something different, you discount it.

Sally was offered the job of head nurse. Everyone said she was ideal for the job but when she thought about taking it, she got sick to her stomach. She said to me, "I want to want the job I'm supposed to want. I just don't want it. But I should still go after it because I can't trust my own feelings."

You need to be able to allow yourself to trust your own judgment. Trust and go with it.

You can also make a mistake. Sometimes you are not sure that your fearful reaction is as much to be trusted as other people's opinions of what is best for you. It is hard to sort that out. One of the ways to sort it out is to take a chance. Either it will work out or it won't. There is nothing wrong with you if you decide that the change or promotion is not enhancing to you. You just need to decide in advance that you will not be stuck. Put the job on probation just as you are put on probation in it. It is hard for anyone to know in advance how a new job will work out. Why should you be any different? You can exhaust yourself making the perfect decision before the fact, and that simply isn't possible.

It is my personal preference to make a decision, be it right or wrong, and learn from it rather than be indecisive and let life happen to me.

I'M AFRAID THAT THEY WILL FIND OUT THAT I AM NOT CAPABLE OF DOING THE JOB.

It really doesn't matter what your skill level is, or what you're doing. If you don't continue to prove yourself, then they will find out what you knew all along and that is that you fooled them, that you really don't know what you're doing.

This is apparent at the college level. The CoA believes that acceptance to college was through a computer error and the 'A's only put off the day of discovery. After all, you really don't know what you're doing, you really don't know what you're talking about. This helps propel you toward a sense of workaholism because you have to constantly keep the pressure on yourself to keep them from finding you out.

I often wonder how employers in this sophisticated era can be so incompetent as to hire people who are not capable of doing the job for which they are hired. And how they make that error mostly with you. Interesting paradox — your manipulative skills are so well developed that they hide the lack of skill on the job. Either your boss is fooled or he is not fooled. If he is fooled, he is foolish enough to continue to believe you are capable. If he is not fooled, he knew what you could do from the beginning.

It's a hard feeling to shake. *Feeling* incapable and *being* incapable are very different. Work on separating that out. The early tape addresses the feeling but job performance addresses more accurately the capability.

I'M AFRAID THAT THEY WILL FIND OUT THAT I'M NOT WORTHY OF HAVING THIS JOB.

The sense of worth, or lack of it, comes from the same thing that many of you feel. *They're* going to find out what a disgusting person you are because you were responsible for whatever terrible things went on in your family. If you hadn't been born, everything would've been fine. Although other people may make mistakes, you **are** a mistake. You were told it often enough and now you believe it.

How stressful this is, particularly in a work situation where you are treated with respect and are valued. This will cause you to distance yourself from those very people who offer you the validation you crave. It creates an approach-avoidance conflict that is excruciating. The excitement of fulfilling the childhood fantasy of getting your needs fulfilled is met head-on with the terror that it is going to blow up in your face because you're unworthy.

IF I SAY NO, I WILL BE REPLACED.

And so you don't say "no". You believe that yours is the one position that they're not going to have any trouble replacing. At the very moment that you say "no", someone will move into your job. You also don't say "no" because of a lack of knowledge of your limitations.

I have clients that don't say "no" to things that are absolutely outrageous. A client of mine went to visit a relative who was three hundred miles away and dying. The boss called her up and said, "Hey, we have a deadline to meet." She came back because she didn't know that she had the right to say "no".

The worst possible outcome of saying "no", because what you are doing has priority, is that you will lose that job. That may not always be the worst possible outcome.

ANYTHING THAT GOES WRONG IS MY FAULT. ANYTHING THAT GOES RIGHT, OF COURSE, IS THE RESULT OF FATE, LUCK OR CHANCE.

And anyone that is unhappy is unhappy with me. This is an emotional response to something that happens in the real world. You know, for example, that the incorrect information in the report was not in your section. You know you were not responsible for it and yet you feel as if you were. You tell yourself that it is crazy for you to feel this way but you can't stop it. The question to ask yourself at this point is: When I was a child, did I get blamed for things that were not my fault? Did I get into trouble when I was nowhere near where the trouble happened? If your answer is "yes", then you know why emotionally you automatically respond as if you have to defend yourself.

A friend of mine called. "You won't believe this", she said. "Try me," I replied.

"I just called my mother and she yelled at me for being over an hour late for lunch. I *know* I had no plans to meet her for lunch but — and here's the kicker — I felt guilty anyway. Does it ever stop?"

Hard to say — certainly beginning to be able to laugh about it helps.

Dismissing those things that go right as, "It was easy" or "Anyone could have done it" or "It goes with the territory" or "I just happened to be there" means that you maintain a low self-image.

You feel bad about what goes badly, regardless of your input and ignore what goes well, still regardless of your input. Sounds like a pretty stuck place to be.

I SHOULD BE ABLE TO DO WHATEVER IS ASKED OF ME.

"After all, why would my employer ask me to do something 'unreasonable'. Since I don't know what 'reasonable' is I get confused."

Maybe, you shouldn't be able to do whatever is asked of you. It is very important for you to learn what requests are reasonable and which are not. The question is not whether or not you are able to fulfill the request but whether it is a request that is appropriate. One main agenda of most of my clients is how they can do less. How can I take on less? How can I make my life less stressful? A man in my supervisory group under 30 years old had a heart attack. There is no reason for that if you can learn how to put things into perspective. And that is learned and that is taught.

Ability is not the key as to whether or not you "should" do it. Nor is — "If I don't do it, no one else will." That's one of the traps of your childhood. Is the request consistent with your job description and is it reasonable? That is all that need be considered. If you consider that and do it anyway, then it is your conscious choice which is different from a "should".

I SHOULDN'T HAVE TO ASK MY BOSS FOR WHAT I NEED.

It sounds like bosses should be clairvoyant simply to reduce your risk of not getting your needs met and having to deal with that. The rationale is "I would be invading his/her space if I asked for what I need." So of course you don't ask. You take care of it yourself whether it's little or whether it's big or whether it's within your domain or whether it's not.

One woman shared that, "When I ask my boss for what I need, I feel shame . . .

"When I asked my mother for what I needed, she would fall apart and I would feel terrible, and I would end up not only not getting my need met but feeling shameful. I had inflicted an additional burden on her. As a result I would end up taking care of her, as well as having to meet my own need."

Asking for help then becomes a very painful experience. Aside from the predictable difficulty of feeling unworthy of someone else's effort and the sense that I *should* be able to handle by myself whatever it is I think I need help with, the fact that my asking will do harm to someone else is what really scares me.

I SHOULD BE ABLE TO FIX UP.

"I should be able to fix anything and everything that goes wrong." After all, that was your tale. You took care of everybody. It is what you know how to do best. "Don't worry I'll . . ." and what happens is that others will let you do it, will often take the credit for what you do, will take you for granted and unless you get angry enough, you will continue to seek approval in this way. "No sweat . . . I'll get the . . . on the way to . . . I'll lay out the money . . . I was staying late anyway . . . Yours doesn't work, take mine."

The Underachiever

Not all CoAs are super responsible, super achievers that have been discredited. Many do not begin to approach their potential. They are held back not by choice but as a response to their childhood tapes. Many of the tapes are the same as for the super achievers but responded to differently.

Sarah, although very capable, goes from one entry-level job to another. She is never satisfied, but that does not change the pattern.

"My mother is a workaholic. All my life people have told me

I'm just like my mother and I hate that. I'm sure that's why I don't try to achieve. I'm terrified that if I did I would fulfill the prophecy and end up just like her."

Tom says, "All I ever heard was, 'You're a failure like your father. — You'll never amount to anything.' I guess I believed it. Why should I bother since it is inevitable that I will fail. After all, if I don't try, I cannot fail."

That is only part of the risk of succeeding. For Tom the greater risk is that he will become an orphan, adrift and alone — cut off from his family.

If he succeeds, it means violating his life script. It means his family were liars and that his life was a lie. In order to continue to be a member of your family you have to play by their rules. That means you *must* fail. If you don't fail, you do not belong. The bonding need is so great that to go it alone and give up that fantasy of getting your needs met is overwhelming.

Then you further judge yourself because you continue in patterns that are self-destructive, even though you "know" better. It has nothing to do with "knowing" better. It has to do with a fear of abandonment.

In the workplace, some of it may come from wanting to be liked and accepted by peers. It is similar to the school-age child who doesn't raise his hand even though he knows the answers so the others won't think of him as a nerd.

There are many who limit their achievement because they will "not give their parents the satisfaction".

"They don't care about me. They only care about what I do. And that is only so they can brag to others about me. They never tell me." This self-defeating behavior comes out of anger at your parents.

"I go fast and then I stop dead in my tracks. I don't take the next step because it feels like I will die if I do — or I'm taking the next step and I'm doing well and then I do something to sabotage myself."

This is a very powerful response to the childhood message of "You will never amount to anything".

The child within you believes that in going against this message you are rejecting your parents. Rejecting them means you are all alone and the child in you is afraid that you cannot survive on your own. So it feels like you are risking death if you continue to grow.

Another variation on this theme is, "All they ever do is nag me about how unsuccessful I am and how well everyone else is doing. I think I don't aspire more just to get back at them."

The reality is that it goes deeper. There is a fear that if they didn't have this to complain about, there would be nothing for them to talk about. In fact, the parents do not want the child to succeed for their own unhealthy reasons and he plays right into their script. It is better to be a loser than to be cut off from the family.

Trying harder, taking aptitude tests, faking it until you make it. These do not work in the long run for the people described here. Support groups and therapy are necessary adjuncts, first to build a new self-concept and then to learn to behave in accordance with it. Those old messages need to be changed and new ones put in their place. That occurs gradually over time with lots of reinforcement and not without pain. The pain that you experience happens at the point where the old tape of worthlessness is at war with the new tape of worthiness. This may exhaust and depress you. Recognize ahead of time that this may happen and resolve to overcome it. You cannot allow the disease to win.

—————CHART A—————

...agement Style	Co-dependent response
...ritical. ...ng is good enough. ... will always be found. ... is withheld.	"I want him/her to like me. Next time, I'll be good enough."
...demanding. ...ps self with work. ...ps employees with ...ts it done in unrealis- ...e.	"He wouldn't ask me to do it if he didn't think I could do it. I'll prove I'm worthy."
...romiser.	"This time he means it."
...aholic or incompetent.	"I need to take care of him/her."
...eaning. ...'re paranoid. You're ...ng a big deal out of ...ng. How can you be ...pid?"	"If I had his/her pressures I'd probably react the same way. He wouldn't say it if there wasn't at least a grain of truth in it."
...ez-faire.	"If I was important enough he'd pay more attention to me. If I don't have full and complete instructions, I'll screw up."
...uing.	"He will understand my pressures and problems and I don't have to worry if I let certain things go."

Chapter Four

CoAs as Supervisors

The issues for the supervisor who is a CoA are very similar, if not the same as for the employee. They just play out somewhat differently. They also affect their subordinates greatly.

These insecurities lead to management styles which tend to perpetuate the alcohol family system.

The behavior becomes alcoholic (drugs need not be present) and the subordinates become co-dependent. You can create co-dependent responses in subordinates who come from typical families, but they will not be as profound as for those who come from dysfunctional families.

CoA supervisors will:

1. Demand Compliance

This is a boundary issue. They become ego involved with their subordinates so they consider any poor performance as a reflection on them.

2. Make Changes Overnight

Even though they are replacing someone who hasn't done anything for two years, and even though they probably have a grace period of three to six months before they are expected to make changes, they will push themselves to redesign an entire program within two weeks. The need is to prove that their appointment was not a mistake, so they put undue pressure on both themselves and their subordinates.

3. Want To Be Liked by Everyone

As a result, they will become over-involved with their subordinates. They will encourage inappropriate self-disclosure and then find themselves in a terrible position when it comes time to rate their job performance. The fear of rejection causes them to put off the appropriate confrontation or to handle them poorly. Things either wait until they get out of hand or little things get blown out of proportion. The need to reprimand is greeted with great anxiety.

4. They Give Away Their Ego to the Organization

This is another example of a boundary issue.

Jean is a middle level manager with a small manufacturing company. She has been home with heart palpitations for the last two weeks and her doctor recommends bed rest for two more. He can find nothing wrong with her heart. She went for a second opinion and the diagnosis was the same: "stress reaction".

During the last quarter of last year the company was in financial trouble. Cuts needed to be made and budgets adjusted to accommodate the difficulty. Jean, a very loyal employee, took those problems on as her own. The company difficulties became hers and the worry totally engulfed her. The company has passed the crisis, but she now pays a personal price. Those that worked to solve the problems but did not become emotionally involved with them are now experiencing relief and personal satisfaction.

5. They Keep Their Personal Feelings Under Control

Since this belief is so strongly held, the lid is kept on all feelings. This is a style that companies support. As a result, managers do not develop their own support systems and "stuff" their reactions. It is not unusual for physical symp-

toms to emerge, such as ulcers
ness in the jaws and throat, coli

6. They Have a Need for Perfectio

This causes them to consider
part of the employees, for inst
tion on them. So they over re
need to be held accountable. T
because the supervisor didn't c
mula to fix it.

Although they delegate resp
be able to let go and over (mi
trust that others will do what t
well enough or they back off c
pensation for their fear.

7. Become Enablers

They tend to feel responsib
"survival" of their subordinate
modate and cover up for poor
subordinates up to have unr
manipulative, lower their job p
added burden on the rest of th

The self-feelings of the worker
supervisor lead to certain managen
on the part of the supervisors and
the worker tend to reproduce the

1) O
   N
   A
   Pr

2) O
   Sv
   Sv
   wc
   Ex
   tic

3) Th

4) W

5) De
   "Y
   m
   no
   so

6) La

7) Re

Chapter Five

BOUNDARIES

One of the legacies of growing up in an alcohol family system is that there is a blurring of boundaries. This leads to confusion in virtually all areas of adult life. In the workplace it affects relationships with supervisors and peers.

The interaction with parents will transfer to the interaction with supervisors. If you grew up with alcoholism, it was hard to tell who was the parent and who was the child. The child not only had to parent him/herself but also, in many cases, had to parent the parents in order to keep the peace so that things would not get out of control and someone get hurt.

As a result, feelings toward authority figures are ambivalent at best. Anger and fear, the need to protect the self, and to anticipate trouble, these feelings arise regardless of the personality of the supervisor. Behaviors of supervisors will be interpreted within this framework with evidence that may or may not be related.

I got a call from my friend Bob, a vice president of our local bank.

"You may like working with these CoAs," he said, "but I frankly don't know if it's worth all the energy. I just had a meeting with my branch manager and I'm still spinning. John came into my office and out of the blue announced that he was upset with me. He said, 'You know how strongly I felt about the schedule changes and you don't care about my feelings!'

"I said, 'Wait a minute! That simply isn't true. I supported the scheduling changes you wanted made *because* I care about your feelings. I don't happen to agree with you but I can understand your point of view and I'm willing to go along.'

"I was completely thrown by what he said. For me, it was a business decision. I was not emotionally invested in it. I can respect points of view other than my own even if I disagree. For me, it was uncomplicated and frankly unimportant in terms of other things that I'm dealing with right now.

"Obviously, it was a big deal for him. He wanted not only my support of his idea but for me to agree that his was the only way to go."

The problem relates to lack of boundaries. The boundaries between him and his idea no longer existed. If Bob didn't agree with his idea, he didn't care about John.

Bob had also become the parent whose approval he always sought and never got. He was playing out his childhood tape of "Do whatever you want — just leave me alone."

Even if the employer is aware of all this, it is not his role to "fix it". If he does that, then he plays into the boundary confusion. His role is to be clear, supportive and consistent. As it happened, Bob got angry because he would not allow himself to be abused and stuffing his feelings would be destructive to him.

Since John sees him as a parent, the anger of his boss also has meaning beyond the interaction. Was he now going to be fired? Did he have to keep a low profile so things wouldn't get worse? Did he have to confront him now about it?

Since the boundaries are so confused, no attention is paid to Bob's position, feelings or reactions and what they mean. The person with boundary confusion gets so caught up in his own feelings and reactions that it is a real struggle to get past them and be aware of what is going on with someone else.

If he can get outside of himself, the branch manager needs to let go of it at this point, because a minor situation is starting to get out of hand. He needs to look at the stuff of the conflict — a change in scheduling design. He wanted the change. The VP was satisfied with the way things were and saw no need for change but would go along with the changes.

The way it progressed was that the situation was not allowed to die. The branch manager wrote Bob a letter about how he reacted to his anger. The VP chose to ignore the letter but couldn't help beginning to question his judgment as to whether this person's value to the organization was as great as he had considered originally. Managers are supposed to put out fires, not start them.

Sibling relationships get distorted as well. Siblings tend to live side by side and although older kids may take care of younger ones, feelings are not shared and meaningful interaction does not take place. There is not a sense of closeness. They live alone together.

Similarly, the peer relationship tends to get confused in the workplace. The desire to get close but the fear of discovery causes ambivalence. The role playing because of the risks of being rejected if you show yourself as you really are — whatever that is — leads to distance. The question of what is safe to talk about and what is not safe to talk about creates confusion. Too much or too little ends up being said. Wanting to be liked will make the CoA overly sensitive to disagreeable co-workers or sexual innuendos. He/she will also be prone to covering up for slackers and not know how much to help out a fellow worker who is behind.

Julia was upset and confused. Her office mate was always late coming back from lunch and coffee breaks. "I'm furious! I end up answering her phone and taking her messages. It's like I'm *her* lousy secretary. I haven't said anything to her yet because I'm afraid I'll lose control or cry. It's like my family. I'm the only one who ever does anything."

The overwhelming nature of the problem exists because of Julia's lack of understanding of boundaries. Her statement about being the "only one who ever does anything" is the clue. Once again, she is taking over as she did as a child. It's the role she knows. If she had a better understanding of boundaries, she wouldn't have a problem. She simply would not answer the other phone. It is not her problem unless she takes it on as her problem. If the phone goes unanswered, it becomes Sandy's problem. She then has to deal with the consequences, not Julia.

The reality is that her lack of understanding of boundaries is what makes it a big issue for her and probably what allows her office mate to take advantage. No problem — Julia will cover, she's a dear.

Sexuality in the Workplace

Many CoAs have been sexually abused as children. This is true for both men and women, although women are generally more aware of the experience. As a result, any hint of sexual harrassment in the workplace causes a very powerful response. Any inappropriate gesture or remark will provoke either a panic or battle response in the CoA.

Although sexual gamesmanship is generally considered undesirable, the CoA will go after the "perpetrator" with a cannon when a pea shooter might have the desired effect. The other extreme of quitting or asking for a transfer may also be an overkill response from childhood.

Needless to say, the promise of promotion for sexual favors is, in and of itself, horrendous enough to warrant whatever power that can be harnessed against it. Such "advances" confuse CoAs who always wonder if they are over-reacting or minimizing when they are told, "Everybody does it! It's not such a big deal." The discussion here is more of the obnoxious office Romeo who propositions everyone to the simple compliment remarking upon, "How well you look today".

Not only is there the early childhood trauma which surfaces in these instances, but also a lack of skill in knowing what to say or how to say it in order to get a point across without creating lifelong ill will.

Many EAP counselors who work with CoAs report that they will tend to have high risk affairs in the workplace. These involve for example, "the married boss". This kind of living on the edge is symptomatic of the CoAs attraction to excitement, stress and chaos. It also plays into the attraction to one who is unavailable so that no real intimacy has to be established. What is established is the fantasy of "he will love me so much that he will leave his wife and we will ride off into the sunset and live happily ever after." Not to worry, though; he won't.

The problem that occurs here is that inevitably either (1) the boss gets bored and ends the affair, (2) belief in the fantasy puts pressure on the relationship and it ends, or (3) the CoA matures and becomes involved with someone available and as a result the work environment goes sour.

This is the point at which help may be sought in the form of: (1) complaint at being passed over, (2) request for transfer, or (3) are referred or fired because of poor job performance.

Once again, the CoA doesn't know what hit her but is certain the problem exists either wholly outside or wholly inside of him/herself.

Consideration must also be given to the CoA who is gay or lesbian. The fears of being found out, the sense of being different, the sense of making yourself up because you don't know who you are — these are symptomatic of being ACoA and are also characteristic of being closeted and gay. They are, therefore, doubly powerful.

One of the significant distinctions that compounds the issue is that much of the fear that the CoA experiences exists only in the emotional world and not in the real world. These fears may lead to certain self-defeating behaviors which create their own consequences but are, for the most part, CoA initiated.

For the gay, the fears of being found out, the sense of being different, the need to manufacture a person because the real you would not be acceptable exist in the real world. "Corporate Homophobia" is a fact of life and gets played out in a variety of subtle and not so subtle ways; so, the person who is gay and also an ACoA, ends up extremely confused. Which is my CoA stuff? Which is my gay stuff? And who the hell am I?

These distinctions need to be addressed by a counselor sensitive to both gay and CoA issues because eventually the lie becomes confused with the truth and the result is disaster.

Chapter Six

CoAs and Workaholism

Workaholism is a condition where the workplace permeates the consciousness to such an extent that it is difficult to concentrate or think about anything other than work. It is different from enjoying your work because it has more of the characteristics of an addiction. Work becomes a high, and withdrawal from it can cause nervousness, anxiety and depression. Family and friends are neglected, and although at first they encourage you and adjust, eventually they exclude you from their lives.

Working hard by active conscious choice is different from what is being discussed here. The concern here is for those who find themselves in a compulsive pattern that is not satisfying to them, who don't know how they got there or how to break the pattern.

The preoccupation with the workplace is set off by the childhood myths discussed in Chapter Three. It can result from other dynamics as well.

From an even broader perspective, an ACoA shares:

When I wonder about how I became a workaholic, it gets pretty clear that it was all part of a process. I didn't set out to be over involved; it just happened. At work I feel loved, accepted, respected and trusted. These are all strong needs of mine. As these feelings grabbed me, I became more secure and developed a deep sense of loyalty. The trust in these feelings developed slowly over these past four years and nine months.

If I label my role here, I see myself as a "family hero". There are several "heroes" here and in some ways we work well together. We're committed to keeping everything running smoothly. We try to anticipate all possible calamities, and we fix the screw-ups. We do have problems working together over issues of control. I have someone who I supervise who is also a strong family hero, and she is the most difficult person of all to supervise.

All the feelings are not good ones. I also feel frustration over poor communications, lack of planning, lack of direction and lack of clear expectations. I feel disappointment that others seem so willing to be so passive. I feel angry at myself when I react to their passivity by becoming more active and intense.

I know intellectually if I were not here, it would all go on and that I don't make the difference, but I don't know how not to react. Because of the love and acceptance I feel, I became very committed to what goes on here. As long as I am here, I have to give it my absolute best.

The problem in all of this is the amount of energy it takes. When I am feeling frustrated or angry, I use up so much energy. I also will start to do a number on myself like "you shouldn't feel this way, you should be grateful", and that moves me nicely into guilt. This depletes me even more.

In these last four years, I've clearly become addicted to this job. I put the bulk of my time, energy, thoughts and emotions into this place. I tell the people I supervise that they and their families come first and then the job, but I don't practice this myself. I've let a lot go in these four years. I don't keep up friendships. I want to "go out" less and less. I've become more introverted, and it seems there's not much that I talk about that isn't work related. I'm boring to me. I've been a supervisor now for one year. As a result, I feel more alone because my peer group is now much smaller. I'm less confident and less sure of myself. I've received positive feedback, but I don't *really accept or believe it.*

I feel panicky at times that I've made the wrong decision to become a supervisor. I've felt despair in that I don't see a positive future here and scared because I don't know what else to do. I feel trapped. Like the alcoholic, everything is slipping away but my addiction to my job. My circle is getting smaller and tighter.

I reached a place where I saw only two alternatives. The first would be to quit; the other was to kill myself. That terrifies me because I don't know what else to do. Fortunately, I don't have such a narrow vision that I don't know there are other alternatives — I just need to identify them.

One thing that I don't really understand yet is how after four years I can do well in my job, be promoted, get good feedback and still feel so unsure of my future and lacking in confidence.

I realize this "family" I work with is in various stages of their own recovery, but I feel I'm slipping backward. I don't know how any of this is coming across. I feel confused, but I am determined to get into a more comfortable place. I do realize that only I can change how I feel. My first goal is to build up my confidence. I want to look at what other alternatives there are and either find a way to get more comfortable here or make whatever change I need to.

Chapter Seven

CoAs and Burnout

Workaholism is the first step toward burnout, and the CoA is a natural candidate for burnout. Not knowing what normal is leads to overdoing and overproving. Not knowing limitations leads to not saying "no". Burnout is a condition where an individual has given more than he has to give. It is a condition where it is felt that there is nothing left.

It is characterized by depression and inability to get out of bed in the morning, in loss of or intense gain in appetite, agoraphobia, a variety of physical symptoms, and substance abuse. For many the issue of burnout is addressed by taking a good hard look at:

1) How much has been taken on?
2) How much of it is necessary?
3) How much of it is unnecessary?
4) What steps can be taken to relieve oneself of unnecessary responsibility?
5) What steps can be taken to relieve oneself of necessary responsibility which may not be necessary in the real world but only in the emotional world.
6) How do I establish priorities?

7) How do I balance a day?

8) How do I prevent relapse?

Most of us burn out *once*. Without intervention, the burn-out pattern for the CoA is to get sick, regroup and then head toward the next burnout.

This happens because:

1) *It's the only way they know how to behave.* With no understanding of or appreciation for moderation, getting sick is the only way not to be in charge. The pattern is predictable.

2) *There are deeper reasons.* Part of the survival struggle that the CoA carries into adulthood propels him/her toward burnout. It is hard for the CoA to believe that they "have made it", and so they continue to play out historical issues.

A high-achieving CoA shares the following feelings in a supervisory group: She has no idea when she begins, that she is about to zero in on why she burns out when she "knows better".

She has been hanging onto her anger at her parents even though they are no longer living. "What's in it for you to stay angry? What is your gain?"

Her answer, profound and painful, makes it clear:

If I hang on to my anger at my parents, I don't have to risk death. If I'm angry, I don't have to risk being close. I don't have to risk growing up. If I grow up and become responsible for myself, I have to give up my search for nurture. I have to take care of myself. Taking care of myself means I will be all alone and if I am all alone, I will die.

So I avoid that by holding onto my anger at my parents as the only route to freedom from them but end up being locked inside me. Owning up to the fact that I don't know how to take care of myself is very hard because I know so clearly how to take care of others.

I do and I don't want to be responsible to and for myself. I want my independence but I still yearn for the nurturing. This is very painful to deal with so I try and reduce the risk of sharing this side of me.

One of the ways that I reduce the risk of being responsible is to take on many responsibilities. If I do that, then I don't have to face myself and no one will know, because I am super responsible, that that is the way I cover my fear. Being super responsible to and for others will effectively hide the fact that I'm ignoring my obligation to myself.

This clearly demonstrates why the usual route is not sufficient. In addition to the tools described earlier, it is imperative that you learn how to:

1) Recognize positive feedback.
2) Acknowledge it.
3) Let it in.

Being offered greater responsibility is positive feedback. It may not be in your best interest to take on more but that does not diminish or dismiss it as a stroke. Separate them out. Be flattered (do it consciously, even if it is not possible to feel it) that you are seen as being capable.

Then make a decision based on what you *want to do*. The compliment of being offered a promotion does not mean you have to accept it.

Learn to recognize your early stress symptoms. *Prevention Magazine* published the following list. Some may be new to you; you may have others to add to it.

At the first sign, *SLOW DOWN*. Yes — easy for me to say; almost as easy as *I TOLD YOU SO*.

Minor Symptoms That May Signal Stress

- ☐ Rashes
- ☐ More colds than normal
- ☐ Hives
- ☐ Memory slips
- ☐ Concentration slides
- ☐ Foot or finger tapping
- ☐ Teeth gnashing, grinding
- ☐ Awaking at 3 a.m. and being unable to fall back asleep
- ☐ Appetite disorders (eat too much or lose appetite)
- ☐ Diarrhea
- ☐ Heart palpitations
- ☐ Eyelid twitching
- ☐ Difficulty falling or staying asleep
- ☐ Minor back pain
- ☐ Sudden bursts of energy
- ☐ Increased sweating
- ☐ More minor accidents than normal
- ☐ Flatulence
- ☐ Frowning/wrinkled forehead
- ☐ Feelings of suspiciousness, worthlessness, inadequacy or rejection
- ☐ Anticipating the worst
- ☐ Nervousness before anything happens
- ☐ Not recognizing a personality shift and refusing to believe it when pointed out
- ☐ Cold hands or feet
- ☐ Halitosis
- ☐ Rapid heartbeat
- ☐ Racing thoughts

- ☐ Feeling trapped
- ☐ Anger, irritation
- ☐ Feeling that things are getting out of control
- ☐ Muscle aches
- ☐ Allergies
- ☐ Jaw pain
- ☐ Minor stomach discomfort
- ☐ Bloated, full feeling
- ☐ Constipation
- ☐ Facial tics, twitches
- ☐ Slight stutter
- ☐ Dry mouth
- ☐ Difficulty swallowing
- ☐ Nausea, vomiting
- ☐ Chronic fatigue
- ☐ Lack of interest in sex
- ☐ Gain/lose weight
- ☐ Menstrual distress
- ☐ Cold, clammy hands
- ☐ Frequent bouts with flu
- ☐ Arthritic joint pain
- ☐ Indecisiveness
- ☐ Frustration
- ☐ Anxiety, panic

If you checked a significant number of items in this list, you may want to evaluate the stress in your life. Remember: What may be a symptom of stress in one person could be nothing more than a normal reaction for someone else. ☐

Chapter Eight

CHANGING JOBS

CoAs do not accept change easily. Change, regardless of its nature involves loss. The sense of self is tentative and for many, the personal identity and the work identity are one and the same; so any change in the workplace is disruptive. It involves the loss of self as it has been understood by the CoA. Many find themselves in tears when things are going well and devastated when things are going poorly. Identification with occupation is not exclusive to CoAs but the exaggerated reaction to change is relevant.

The leaving is stressful to the CoA because:

1) Leaving is a sign of disloyalty, so the CoA will experience guilt.
2) The CoA believes that the former colleagues:
   — "Will be angry with me"
   — "Won't like me any more"
   — "Will punish me"
   and that the new colleagues
   — "Will reject me, so I will be all alone in a hostile environment."
3) If the CoA takes care of him or herself, something terrible will happen to others.

— "Those under my protection will be thrown to the wolves." — Survivor guilt.

For many the leaving is more difficult than the new start. That is not only because of the struggles involved in leaving but because focusing on the leaving also serves as a smokescreen to avoid the fears involved in the change.
They include:

1) Fear of success
2) Fear of failure

Much has been written about the female fear of success (nice girls don't) and the male fear of failure (if you're a man, you will) and those culturally defined fears exist for the CoA as well. In and of themselves the messages of "You'll never get a man" or "The world will know you're a wimp", can cause you great anxiety.

However, for the CoA the underlying message of *you're not worthy* and the unconscious belief in that message causes panic when one goes against it.

The decision to change jobs for a CoA is excruciating.

Decision-making skills are lacking. There is no frame of reference for making a careful, thought out decision without help.

As a result job changes will:

1) Happen to the CoA, rather than result from the CoA making the decision, and
2) CoAs will make impulsive decisions and live with the results of those impulses.

    It is not unusual for a CoA to get stuck in trying to make a decision. This comes from forward and backward projection and an inability or lack of understanding of necessary steps in the moment.
3) Since leaving is so hard, it has to be the *perfect* job. It has to be the right location, the right title, the right job description, the right salary, the right perks, the right opportunity for advancement, the right assistance — in short, everything. Otherwise, why bother? The agonizing over leaving means that the new job is a "life-long" commitment. The idea that the company might change, that you

might change or that what is ideal for you today may not be ideal tomorrow is too complicated a notion to enter the picture.

4) Learning involves risk. This brings up the childhood fear, "If I take a risk and it's a mistake, my parents will humiliate me, mock me out and make fun of me to their friends." The memory of that torture is excruciating.

In general, people look for new jobs because:
1) They are unsatisfied where they are,
2) A growth opportunity presents itself,
3) It is time to move on for one's own development, and
4) Circumstances intervene.

CoAs look for new jobs when:

1) **The present situation becomes intolerable.** Dissatisfaction is generally rationalized or dismissed, or blamed on self. Subsequently, the discomfort builds until the situation is intolerable. Then another job must be found or the CoA will act out or get fired. The result is that the search is done with great urgency and a new position becomes more the luck of the draw than a carefully selected choice — like the individual who marries in order to get out of the house. This rapid choice is a good way for setting up the same situation all over again.

2) **Even though the CoA complains that he/she is under-appreciated and under-utilized, growth opportunities are not met with enthusiasm and an inner self-validation.** They are met with fear of discovery on the one hand and the suspicion that the growth opportunity is not all that it appears to be on the other. Since most new opportunities are not all they're purported to be, looking at the negative side helps to allay the inadequacy fears. It is a sign of growth for the CoA to address concerns directly and discuss terms. It is more usual to "stuff" concerns, put off the decision, panic that someone else will be offered the job and end up accepting the job on the employer's terms. Losing the opportunity as the result of avoidance is an alternate possibility and leads to an initial sense of relief. Then the fantasy of "if only" sets in.

3) **CoAs rarely move on solely because it is time to go further.** This comes from an inability to generalize skills. "I may do fine where I am but could I make it somewhere else?" Jobs are not looked on as opportunities to demonstrate particular skills but as a self definition.

Moving on because it is time is a carefully thought out and calculated decision. It involves preparation and planning and deliberate systematic action. This is contrary to the operational mode of the CoA who operates best under pressure and in crisis.

4) **CoAs change jobs when circumstances intervene.** Getting fired has the same devastation for CoAs as it does for others. Rejection, regardless of whether the job was worth having, brings up insecurities, and people respond with either depression, which debilitates, or anger, which energizes. CoAs are less prone than others to be able to use anger on their own behalf. It has been such a destructive force in the past that it is hard to harness it and make it useful. The knowledge of how to use anger and the freedom to see anger as being creative is not available to the CoA.

Other circumstances, such as company moves or family crises, are managed extremely well by CoAs. They are calm in the crisis and are able to do what needs to be done. Where others may fall apart in crisis and not be able to think clearly, CoAs become energized and clear thinking. This is one benefit of the legacy of living from crisis to crisis in childhood.

Chapter Nine

THE OVERVIEW

The general picture of the ACoA is true in every aspect of life. An overview of basic characteristics of the ACoA as they relate to the workplace is therefore appropriate to look at.

Basic Characteristics of CoAs in the Workplace

Adult children of alcoholics guess at what normal is.

The significance of this statement cannot be overestimated, as it is their most profound characteristic. Adult children of alcoholics simply have no experience with what is normal.

After all, when you take a look at your history, how could you have any understanding of normalcy? Your home life varied from slightly mad to extremely bizarre.

Since this was the only home life you knew, what others would consider "slightly mad" or "extremely bizarre" were usual to you. If there was an occasional day that one could characterize as "normal", it certainly was not typical, and therefore could not have had much meaning.

Beyond your chaotic day-to-day life, part of what you did

was to live in fantasy. You lived in a world that you created all your own, a world of what life would be like IF . . . what your home would be like IF . . . the way your parents would relate to each other IF . . . the things that would be possible for you IF . . . And you structured a whole life based on something that was probably impossible. The unrealistic fantasies about what life would be like if your parent got sober probably helped you survive, but these added to your confusion as well.

It becomes very clear that you have no frame of reference for what it is like to be in a normal household. You also have no frame of reference for what is O.K. to say and to feel. In a more typical situation, one does not have to walk on eggs all the time. One doesn't have to question or repress one's feelings all the time. Because you did, you became confused. Many things from the past contributed to your having to guess at what normal is.

What this means in the workplace is that CoAs are:

1) Ideal candidates for exploitation because they don't know when to say "no!"

2) Very frequently scapegoated because they ask a million questions.

3) Will pick inappropriate role models because they make assumptions and don't check them out.

Adult children of alcoholics have difficulty in following a project through from beginning to end.

The topic one evening in an adult children of alcoholics' meeting was procrastination. When I asked the group members to talk about what it meant to them, the opening response was, "I'm the world's biggest procrastinator", or "Somehow I just don't seem to be able to finish anything that I start".

These comments are fairly typical, and it's not too hard to understand why a difficulty exists. These people are not procrastinators in the usual sense.

The great job was always around the corner. The big deal was always about to be made. The work that needed to be done around the house would be done in no time . . . the toy that will be built . . . the go-cart . . . the doll house . . . and on and on.

"I'm going to do this, I'm going to do that." But this or that never really happened. Not only didn't it happen, but the alcoholic wanted credit simply for having the idea, even for intending to do it. You grew up in this environment.

There were many wonderful ideas, but they were never acted on. If they were, so much time passed that you had forgotten about the original idea.

Who took the time to sit down with you when you had an idea for a project and said, "That's a good idea. How are you going to go about doing it? How long is it going to take you? What are the steps involved?" Probably no one. When was it that one of your parents said, "Gee, that idea is terrific! You sure you can do it? Can you break it down into smaller pieces? Can you make it manageable?" Probably never.

This is not to suggest that ALL parents who do not live with alcohol teach their children how to solve problems. But it is to suggest that in a functional family the child has this behavior and attitude to model. The child observes the process and the child may even ask questions along the way. The learning may be more indirect than direct, but it is present. Since your experience was so vastly different, it should be no surprise that you have a problem with following a project through from beginning to end. You haven't seen it happen and you don't know how to make it happen. Lack of knowledge isn't the same as procrastination.

What this means in the workplace is that CoAs:
1) Are shortsighted.
2) Will operate superbly under pressure.
3) Will be unable to complete long-term projects.

Adult children of alcoholics lie when it would be just as easy to tell the truth.

Lying is basic to the family system affected by alcohol. It masquerades in part as overt denial of unpleasant realities, coverups, broken promises, and inconsistencies. It takes many forms and has many implications. Although it is somewhat different from the kind of lying usually talked about, it certainly is a departure from the truth.

The first and most basic lie is the family's denial of the problem, so the pretense that everything at home is in order is a lie, and the family rarely discusses the truth openly, even with each other. Perhaps somewhere in one's private thoughts there is a recognition of the truth, but there is also the struggle to deny it.

The next lie, the cover-up, relates to the first one. The non-alcoholic family member covers up for the alcoholic member. As a child, you saw your non-alcoholic parent covering up for your alcoholic parent. You heard him or her on the phone making excuses for your mother or father for not fulfilling an obligation, not being on time. That's part of the lie that you lived.

You also heard a lot of promises from your alcoholic parent. These, too, turned out to be lies.

Lying as the norm in your house became part of what you knew and what could be useful to you. At times, it made life much more comfortable. If you lied about getting your work done, you could get away with being lazy for a while. If you lied about why you couldn't bring a friend home, or why you were late coming home, you could avert unpleasantness. It seemed to make life simpler for everybody.

Lying has become a habit. That's why the statement, "Adult children of alcoholics lie when it would be just as easy to tell the truth," is relevant. But if lying is what you have heard comes naturally, perhaps it is not as easy to tell the truth.

In this context, "It would be just as easy to tell the truth", means that you derive no real benefit from lying.

What this means in the workplace is that CoAs:

1) Second-guess the person who asks so that they can give the answer they *think* the person wants.
2) Will agree to perform tasks they cannot perform although they assume that they *should* be able to do them or they would not have been asked.

Adult children of alcoholics judge themselves without mercy.

When you were a child, there was no way that you were

good enough. You were constantly criticized. You believed that your family would be better off without you, because you were the cause of the trouble. You may have been criticized for things that made no sense. "If you weren't such a rotten kid, I wouldn't have to drink." It makes no sense, but if you hear something often enough, for a long enough period of time, you will end up believing it. As a result, you internalized these criticisms as negative self-feelings. They remain, even though no one is saying them to you anymore.

Since there is no way for you to meet the standards of perfection that you have internalized from childhood, you are always falling short of the mark you have set for yourself. As a child, whatever you did was not quite good enough. No matter how hard you tried, you should have tried harder. If you got an A, it should have been an A+. You were never good enough. A client told me that his mother was so demanding that when he was in basic training, he found the sergeants loose. So this became a part of you . . . who you are, a part of the way you see yourself. The "shoulds" and "should nots" can become paralyzing after a while.

Your judgment of others is not nearly as harsh as your judgment of yourself, although it is hard for you to see other people's behavior in terms of a continuum either. Black and white, good or bad, are typically the way you look at things. Either side is an awesome responsibility. You know what it feels like to be bad, and how those feelings make you behave. And then if you are good, there is always the risk that it won't last. So either way, you set yourself up. Either way there is a great amount of pressure on you all of the time. How difficult and stressful life is. How hard it is to just sit back and relax and say, "It's O.K. to be me."

What this means in the workplace is that CoAs:

1) Will assume that they are responsible for anything that goes wrong.

2) Will not accept strokes if the task was easy to accomplish.

3) Will downplay any credit they receive for completing a difficult task because "it's all a part of the job".

Adult children of alcoholics have difficulty having fun.

What this means in the workplace is that CoAs have difficulty separating themselves from the job.

Adult children of alcoholics take themselves very seriously.

These two characteristics are very closely linked. If you're having trouble having fun, you're probably taking yourself very seriously, and if you don't take yourself all that seriously, chances are you can have fun.

Once again, in order to understand this problem, you need to look back at your childhood. How much fun was your childhood? You don't have to answer that. Children of alcoholics simply don't have much fun. One child of an alcoholic described it as "chronic trauma". You didn't hear your parents laughing and joking and fooling around. Life was a very serious, angry business. You didn't really learn to play with the other kids. You could join in some of the games, but were you really able to let yourself go and have fun? Even if you could have, it was discouraged. The tone around the house put a damper on your fun. Eventually, you just went along with everyone else. Having fun just wasn't fun. There was no place for it in your house. You gave it up. It just wasn't a workable idea. The spontaneous child within was squashed.

Having fun, being silly, being child-like, is to be foolish. It is no wonder that adult children of alcoholics have difficulty having fun. Life is too serious.

You also have trouble separating yourself from your work, so you take yourself very seriously at whatever job you have to do. You can't take the work seriously and not yourself. You are therefore a prime candidate for burnout.

One night a client turned to me with a very angry face and said, "You may make me laugh at myself, but I want you to know I don't think it's funny."

What this means in the workplace is that for the CoA the intensity from childhood carries over into the workplace and everything is taken **very** seriously.

Adult children of alcoholics have difficulty with intimate relationships.

They want very much to have healthy, intimate relationships, but it is extraordinarily difficult for a number of reasons:

The first and most obvious reason is that they have no frame of reference for a healthy, intimate relationship because they have not seen one. The only model they have is their parents, which you and I know was not healthy.

They also carry with them the experience of "come close, go away," the inconsistency of a loving parent-child relationship. They feel loved one day and rejected the next. The fear of being abandoned is a terrible fear they grow up with. If the fear isn't overwhelming, it certainly gets in the way. Not knowing what it is like to have a consistent, day-to-day, healthy, intimate relationship with another person makes building one very painful and complicated.

The fear of abandonment gets in the way of the developing of a relationship. The development of any healthy relationship requires a lot of give and take and problem-solving. There is always some disagreement and anger which a couple resolve. A minor disagreement gets very big very quickly for adult children of alcoholics, because the issue of being abandoned takes precedence over the original issue.

These overwhelming fears of being abandoned or rejected prevent any ease in the process of developing a relationship. Coupled with a sense of urgency, "This is the only time I have; if I don't do it now, it will never happen," tend to put pressure on the relationship. It makes it much more difficult to evolve slowly, to let two people get to know each other better, and to explore each other's feelings and attitudes in a variety of ways.

This sense of urgency makes the other person feel smothered, even though it is not the intent. I know a couple who have tremendous problems because whenever they argue, she panics and worries that he is now going to leave her. She needs constant reassurance in the middle of the argument that he's not going to leave her, and that he still loves her. When he is in conflict, which is difficult for him as well, he tends to want to withdraw and be by himself. Needless to say, this makes the issue at hand more difficult to resolve than if it were only the issue itself needing to be confronted.

The feelings of being insecure, of having difficulty in trusting, and questions about whether or not you're going to get hurt are not exclusive to adult children of alcoholics. These are problems most people have. Few people enter a relationship fully confident that things are going to work out the way they hope they will. They enter a relationship hopeful, but with a variety of fears.

So, all of the things that cause you concern are not unique to you. It's simply a matter of degree; your being a child of an alcoholic caused the ordinary difficulties to become more severe.

What this means in the workplace is that:

1) CoAs have trouble with boundaries so don't know how much and what information about themselves to share with fellow workers and supervisors.

2) They will not know how to assess what is a compliment and what is exploitation — be it sexual harassment or a personal favor.

Adult children of alcoholics over react to changes over which they have no control.

This is very simple to understand. The young child of the alcoholic was not in control. The alcoholic's life was inflicted on him, as was his environment.

In order to survive when growing up, he needed to turn that around. He needed to begin taking charge of his environment. This became very important and remains so. The child of the alcoholic learns to trust himself more than anyone else when it's impossible to rely on someone else's judgment.

As a result, you are very often accused of being controlling, rigid and lacking in spontaneity. This is probably true. It doesn't come from wanting to do everything your own way. It isn't because you are spoiled or unwilling to listen to other ideas. It comes from the fear that if you are not in charge, if a change is made abruptly, quickly and without your being able to participate in it, you will lose control of your life.

When you look back on your reaction and your behavior

later, you feel somewhat foolish, but at the time you were simply unable to shift gears.

What this means in the workplace is that for the CoA:

1) Any change involves some loss of one's identity.
2) Adjustment to change involves experiencing the old fears of inadequacy and discovery.

Adult children of alcoholics constantly seek approval and affirmation.

We talk about an external and an internal locus of control. When a child is born, the environment pretty much dictates how he is going to feel about himself. The school, the church, and other people all have influence, but the most important influence is what we call "significant others". In the child's world, this means his parents. So the child begins to believe who he is by the messages that he gets from his parents. And as he gets older these messages become internalized and contribute significantly to his self-image. The movement is toward the internal locus of control.

The message that you got as a child was very confused. It was not unconditional love. It was not, "I think you're terrific, but I'm not too happy about what you just did." The definitions were not clear and the messages were mixed. "Yes, no, I love you, go away." So you grew up with some confusion about yourself. The affirmations you didn't get on a day-to-day basis as a child, you interpret as negative.

Now, when affirmation is offered, it's very difficult to accept. Accepting the affirmation would be the beginning of changing one's self-image.

What this means in the workplace is that:

1) Since the CoAs cannot affirm themselves, they look for it from supervisors and co-workers.
2) They will overwork in order to get strokes.
3) They become convinced that the next promotion will provide personal validation.

Adult children of alcoholics feel that they are different from other people.

They also assume that in any group of people everyone else

feels comfortable and they are the only ones who feel awkward. This is not peculiar to them. Never, of course, does
anyone check it out and find out that each person has his own
way of trying not to look awkward. Is that true of you, too?

Interestingly enough, you even feel different in a group of
adult children of alcoholics. Feeling different is something you
have had with you since childhood and even if the circum-
stance does not warrant it, the feeling prevails. Other children
had an opportunity to be children. You didn't. You were very
much concerned with what was going on at home. You could
never be completely comfortable playing with other children.
You could not be fully there. Your concerns about your home
problems clouded everything else in your life.

What happened to you is what happened to the rest of your
family. You became isolated. As a result, socializing, being a
part of any group, became increasingly difficult. You simply
did not develop the social skills necessary to feel comfortable
or a part of the group.

It is hard for children of alcoholics to believe that they can
be accepted because of who they are, and that the acceptance
does not have to be earned.

What this means in the workplace is that CoAs will comply
with any requests and demands, regardless of how appropriate
or inappropriate they are, because they don't want to be discovered as being different.

Adult children of alcoholics are either super responsible or super irresponsible.

Either you take it all on, or you give it all up. There is no
middle ground. You tried to please your parents, doing more
and more, or you reached the point where you recognized it
didn't matter, so you did nothing. You also did not see a family
that cooperated with each other. You didn't have a family that
decided on Sunday, "Let's all work in the yard. I will work on
this, and you work on that, and then we'll come together."

Not having a sense of being a part of a project, of how to
cooperate with other people and let all the parts come
together and become a whole, you either do all of it, or you do
none of it. You also don't have a good sense of your own

limitations. Saying "no" is extraordinarily difficult for you, so you do more and more and more. You do it — not because you really have a bloated sense of yourself — you do it (1) because you don't have a realistic sense of your capacity, or (2) because if you say "no" you are afraid that they will find you out. They will find out that you are incompetent. The quality of the job you do does not seem to influence your feelings about yourself. So you take on more and more and more . . . until you finally burn out.

What this means in the workplace is that:

1) CoAs have difficulty sharing responsibility since they have no experience with operating in a cooperative atmosphere; so, they take it all on or back away entirely.
2) They find it difficult to trust that others will do what they have agreed to do.
3) They may judge the performances of others and the organization in the same merciless way they judge themselves.

Adult children of alcoholics are extremely loyal, even in the face of evidence that the loyalty is undeserved.

The alcoholic home appears to be a very loyal place. Family members hang in long after reasons dictate that they should leave. The so-called "loyalty" is more the result of fear and insecurity than anything else; nevertheless, the behavior that is modeled is one where no one walks away just because the going gets rough. This sense enables the adult child to remain in involvements that are better dissolved.

Since making a friend or developing a relationship is so difficult and so complicated, once the effort has been made it is permanent. If someone cares enough about you to be your friend, your lover, or your spouse, then you have the obligation to stay with them forever. If you have let them know who you are, if they have discovered who you are and not rejected you, that fact, in and of itself, is enough to make you sustain the relationship. The fact that they may treat you poorly does not matter. You can rationalize that. Somehow, no matter what they do, or say, you can figure out a way to excuse their behavior and find yourself at fault. This reinforces your negative self-image and enables you to stay in the relationship. Your loyalty is unparalleled.

What this means in the workplace is that:

1) "If they were kind enough to hire me, I owe them my loyalty."
2) The CoA will give loyalty immediately and automatically.

Adult children of alcoholics are impulsive.

They tend to lock themselves into a course of action without giving serious consideration to alternative behaviors or possible consequences. This impulsivity leads to confusion, self-loathing, and loss of control over their environment. In addition, they spend an excessive amount of energy cleaning up the mess.

As a child you could not predict the outcome of any given behavior, so you don't know how to do it now. Also there was no consistency at home. As a result, you haven't the following framework of "When I behaved impulsively in the past, this happened and that happened and this person reacted in that way." Sometimes it would go O.K., and sometimes it wouldn't. Essentially, it may not have really mattered. Nor did anyone say to you, "These are the possible consequences of that behavior. Let's talk about other things that you might do."

What this means in the workplace is that:

1) CoAs have difficulty with decision-making so will behave impulsively.
2) Since separation issues are so difficult, they will tend to move on quickly rather than deal with them.

PART TWO

DEVELOPING
HEALTHY
PATTERNS

The problem has been stated. The complexities have been exposed. The next question is what can be done about it? Or as the typical CoA would say, "Is there any hope?"

The answer is a simple — Yes. There is hope and YES — there is a great deal that can be done about it.

This section of the book contains the "How to" of unhooking from the past and living in the present, all the while being mindful of the future.

Chapter Ten

Developing Healthy
Workplace Relationships

I would encourage you to begin thinking in terms of how to make things different. You can dwell forever on the pain. It is important to take a real good look at your issues, bring them out, chew them up, and spit them out, know that they'll come up again from time to time, and go on. You need to dwell on how you're going to make it different; what you're going to do in order to feel different in practical kinds of ways. What follows is a practical list.

KNOW YOUR PERFORMANCE STYLE

Either accept it, work with it, or work to change it.

Many of you learned to do things under pressure because that was your life experience. You went from crisis to crisis. Nobody taught you how to do things systematically. Nobody said, "You need to spend an hour a night on your homework." So when you were in school, for example, if you got your paper in at all, you did it the night before. And now you have a deadline at work, even if you have had plenty of lead time, you probably do it the night before.

Then you come down on yourself deciding that there's something wrong with you because you always leave things to the last minute.

That may be the way you work best. So rather than make the decision that something is wrong with you, recognize that this is the way you perform. *Acccept it!*

If you have a history of getting things done when they're supposed to be done, don't automatically decide that you're doing it the wrong way. Know your performance style. It is important to know that about yourself. Different people operate differently and your early experiences may have taught you to operate best under pressure. It may have become your performance style. Concern yourself with it only if it's **not** working for you. Don't fix what's working, or as a colleague says, you don't fix what isn't broken.

BE AWARE OF YOUR PRIORITIES AND LIVE BY THEM

Not rigidly, but mindfully. CoAs tend to give everything equal priority. Getting the wash done has the same priority as, say, filing your income tax. Life consists of many chores, obligations and projects. If each one has equal priority, it is very easy to become overwhelmed by all of them. Not *everything* has to be done immediately but some things have to. Not *everything* has to be completed immediately but rather has to be held to manageable levels. If prioritizing is one of your difficult areas, you may need help with it.

The first thing you need to do is make a list of the things you have to do and give them a 1, 2 or 3 as a priority. If you have trouble doing this, ask your boss what needs to be done and when.

If you have time when you have completed the 1s, then do some of the 2s. Make this list every day. It will help to give you a handle on things. Otherwise, it is too easy to feel overwhelmed and panic. Those feelings take a lot of energy and will drain you to the point that you are only able to accomplish very little and that feeds the panic.

DISCOVER YOUR LIMITATIONS AND LIVE REALISTICALLY WITHIN THEM.

You cannot do everything. We all have limitations. It is important to know that recognizing your limitations is not a way to put yourself down. Rather, it is a way to set realistic parameters to your work life. Become aware of your assets and respect them. You may not be able to feel good about them but you can be cognizant of them.

Be sure of your job description. It should be in writing. That way, you can know what your employer expects of you and you can begin to determine what is reasonable to expect of yourself. If the demands on you are far different from your job description, it is important for you to find out what that means.

With a sense of your limitations, both personal and in terms of your job, you can then do some realistic goal setting. You can then define some parameters and become more secure in your work life. You can determine your direction and begin to develop a systematic way to get there.

LEARN MEDITATION, SELF-HYPNOSIS OR SOMETHING ALONG THIS LINE AS A WAY OF REDUCING STRESS.

This is absolutely essential.

Since so many of you are drawn to high stress occupations, it becomes very important to find ways of managing the stress. A relaxation technique, practiced on a daily basis, needs to become part of your lifestyle. If you don't practice it on a daily basis and it does not become a habit, you will not be able to draw on it when you need it.

Not only is this useful for reducing stress, it will help you to be more creative. Ideas that have no room to surface in a flooded mind or in a mind that is being outer-directed can come to the fore during meditation.

Many of the stress-related illnesses that you are prone to can be minimized if not avoided entirely.

SEPARATE THE BEING FROM THE DOING

It's a complicated idea. What happens is that when someone criticizes your work, you take it as a criticism of yourself.

A counselor that I know came in to see me, devastated

because a woman said, "I am leaving your therapy group because I can get the same stuff from Al-Anon." He began by defending himself. "You know", he said, "I've been a therapist for ten years and this hasn't happened to me before. I know I'm competent."

These are his words but not his feelings. He didn't react to her in terms of his competence. If he had reacted to her in terms of his competence, then he could have explored with her what it was about the group experience that she found lacking and learn from it.

What he reacted to instead was from an earlier time. What he heard was his father saying, "You'll never amount to anything." We had to address what went on in *his* self-esteem first in order for him to learn and change in the doing. When he recognized the tape he was playing in his head was old and not accurate, he could then separate from it and look at the criticism in a new light. This happens over and over. Be careful when someone criticizes you for what you do that you take a look at it in terms of what you have done, *not* in terms of who you are. And if they criticize you in terms of who you are, then it is important for you to assess carefully whether or not this is a work situation that is beneficial for you to be in. None of us need to be in a situation where our person is being judged.

BUILD IN TIME FOR YOURSELF.

It is essential for you to have factors in your life other than work. Family, friends, hobbies and the like need to be part of your life.

If work is your whole life and the only place where your needs are met, you put yourself at risk. The loss of a job, a new boss who is difficult to work with, or job dissatisfaction will be far more devastating than if you have other interests. Your entire identity should not be defined by your occupation. Loss of job need not be equaled with loss of self if you take proper safeguards.

Building in time for yourself can also mean creating "non-productive" time. Taking a bath, reading a novel, going for a walk, listening to music, riding a bike, etc. — these all fall into that category. Build it in on a daily basis. Put it in ink on your daily calendar and be as conscientious to the self-commitment as you are to your commitment to others.

LEARN WHAT IS APPROPRIATE AND WHAT IS INAPPROPRIATE TO SHARE IN THE WORK SETTING.

Though you feel close to others that you work with, this does not mean that it is appropriate to tell them personal things. CoAs, because of the boundary issues, tend to confuse this. An employer who comes to me for supervision asked my assessment of someone she had just interviewed. "You know, I really want to hire her, but during our interview she said, 'If I appear a little nervous it's because I just came from my doctor and he says I may have herpes.' "

That was inappropriate to share with a potential employer. It started the potential employer questioning what she is going to share and what is she not going to share on the job. "I'm going to be sending this individual into schools. She's going to be developing relationships in those schools and I'm concerned about what she will say."

It is not a good idea to share your fears and concerns with your employer. No matter how good the relationship is, your employer has got to be concerned about your job performance if you tell her how panicked you are that you won't be able to make it financially after the divorce, how you have had three sleepless nights in a row because your son comes in very late and very drunk. Your employer may care about you and your well being, but that is not the relationship where disclosure of this nature is in your best interest.

LEARN TO LEAVE THE FANTASY OUT OF THE WORKPLACE. LEARN HOW TO ASSESS REALISTICALLY WHAT IS HAPPENING.

It goes something like this: because it's real easy for you, you get caught up in the fantasy. You need to assess realistically when your boss says, "I know I didn't give you the raise I promised, but in six months things are really gonna change," or, "I know the office is not what it's supposed to be but when we expand . . ." Be really careful about how easily you get sucked into this kind of stuff. "I am asking you now to take on this additional responsibility but it's not permanent." Watch it. Watch it.

Wishing doesn't make it so. It didn't as a child and it doesn't now. The difference is that as a child you had few options. As an adult you're in a different position. You can set a deadline for yourself. You can discover what control you have over seeing that desired changes occur. Then you live in the real world and take charge of yourself regardless of what flights of fancy are going on around you.

DON'T GUESS; CHECK THINGS OUT

Guessing is one of the things you learned to do best as children. You never learned to check things out; you never learned to ask. You never learned to question. But you really need to check things out. Things may not be as they appear because you're seeing it only from your personal frame of reference, so it's very important to ask if you're not sure. If you decide that somebody is angry at you, ask why. It may be important for you to know. And who knows? It might not even have anything to do with you.

A man I know came to see me very disturbed because someone was no longer saying hello to him in the morning. He couldn't figure out what he had done to offend this person and didn't know how to handle it. "What do I do about it? Do I confront him? Do I ignore him? Do I let it go? I'm lost and I don't want to make things worse."

"Are you the only one he's not saying good morning to?" I asked. He thought for a minute and then said, "Come to think of it, he's not greeting anybody."

The possibility is very strong that it may not have to do with you. It may have to do with him. Checking things out quite often takes the sting out of it. It helps you to begin to look at things realistically. Workplace rumors need to be checked out. Somehow, the walls have ears but quite often the ears are clogged.

Mary, after a week of near desperation, finally went to her boss with a rumor she had heard. "I hear through the grapevine that you are looking to replace me and I thought I was doing a good job." She struggled to hold back the tears.

"I was hoping to save this announcement for the staff meeting and surprise you," he said. "Your promotion has come through. Congratulations."

Before you approach your boss or co-workers, it is a good idea to check things out with a person or support group who cares about your best interest. You may need help in determining the appropriateness and style of presentation.

Although different circumstances may call for different strategies the principle remains the same. Check things out. Don't guess.

OVER REACTION IS HISTORICAL. LEARN TO SEPARATE THE HISTORY FROM THE MOMENT

If you find that something is really making you nuts, it probably doesn't have to do with the given situation. It probably relates back to something that happened in your childhood and the person in question has become someone else to you. It is important before you act or react on the basis of that to figure out who that person is.

June's boss called her and said, " 'I need to see you. I have some bad news.' I panicked inside. Oh my God! What have I done! What is going to happen to me? How can I cover myself? The panic was overwhelming. By the time I got to his office I was a basket case. He took one look at me and realized he had alarmed me. 'I'm sorry', he said. 'The problem has nothing to do with you. I just need your input on how to explain to the staff that I'm not going to be able to offer the salary increases that I had projected.' " Her over reaction was a direct result of her childhood. Anything that went wrong became her responsibility to fix, regardless of whether she had any part in its going wrong or whether she had any idea of how to fix it.

Chapter 11

FINDING THE RIGHT JOB FOR YOU

Part of your growth may involve realizing that the job you hold may not be the right job for you. It is important to recognize that changing jobs involves a process. It is the same process for everyone, regardless of whether or not they grew up in a dysfunctional family. There are steps in the process that CoAs may not be aware of:

1. *Have an up-to-date resume, regardless of whether or not you are satisfied with your employment.* It will give you an opportunity to explore whatever may come along and interest you — even tangentially.

   a) If you do not know how to do a resume, pick up a book on the subject and follow those guidelines. Nobody automatically knows how to do it until they have done it the first time.

   b) Have someone you trust look it over for typos or additional thoughts.

2. *You may or may not be suited for the work you are doing and may be very confused as to what to do about it.* Having defined yourself by other's opinions and trying to believe that they are your own is most perplexing.

a) Take an interest inventory to see where they lie.
b) Take some aptitude tests and see where your potential lies.
c) Take a personality profile to find out your interactive style.

This will give you an objective assessment of your ideal work profile and then you can explore the options. There are some good books on this subject. *What Color is Your Parachute?* is among the most readable.

Learn about the process of job change and try and set up an orderly system for yourself — step by step — with a reasonable time frame.

You may feel that others have the edge when it comes to parenting and intimate relationships because they may have good role models, but in the marketplace, as uneasy and insecure as you feel, you have the better survival skills. It is a great leveler.

Chapter Twelve

CoAs as Counseling Professionals

CoAs make fine counseling professionals. Indeed many CoAs, as we have seen, are involved in the field. This discussion does not relate to inadequacy on their part but rather the pitfalls many experience at work as counselors. It relates to their self-feelings and how they get in the way of feeling good about the job that they do.

Children of alcoholics have very well developed gut responses. This is a survival skill they learn as children. Words are not as meaningful to them as they are to other people. They can get their clues not only from the words but from a variety of other sources. They are able to gain a sense of what their client is feeling and where their client is at without going into lengthy descriptions which very often get in the way of knowing what is really going on. Since these gut reactions are so basic as to be almost instinctual, it is difficult to even explain how you know. Counseling is one area where identification with childhood trauma can add to one's expertise — unfortunate, but true.

CHILDREN OF ALCOHOLICS WHO ARE PROFESSIONALS VERY OFTEN SEE THEMSELVES AS FRAUDS.

It is not unusual for the CoA counselor to believe that he or she is a fraud. It has far more to do with self-feelings than with performance.

Someone I supervise came to me with this issue not too long ago. "How can I help my clients build their self-esteem if I struggle with that myself?" he said.

The idea that unless all of your personal issues are resolved, you are counseling under false pretenses would mean that no one would be qualified to be a counselor.

If your client's issue is your own current struggle, you may need to refer him or her to someone else. Counselors need to be human and not being finished is a part of being human.

Most of us from time to time when faced with new situations that involve the demonstration of confidence feel like "little kids playing grown up." It is that child within us that has the performance anxiety.

The fear of the CoA is deeper and each workplace job performance assessment brings it up all over again. "How long will it be until they discover I've been fooling them into believing that I know what I'm doing?" This leaves the CoA in a continual state of stress.

ADULT CHILDREN OF ALCOHOLICS TEND TO OVER IDEN-TIFY WITH AND BECOME OVER INVESTED IN THEIR CLIENTS.

This is a boundary issue which relates directly back to childhood. It was impossible to know where your needs and feelings ended and someone else's began. It was impossible to know who was the parent and who was the child. To what degree were you supposed to make it right for everyone else? How could you know what was your problem and what was somebody else's? It's very easy to become overly concerned with your clients as well.

It is not to the client's benefit to bring concerns about him or her home with you night after night. It does not improve your skill as a counselor not to be able to leave your clients behind. The client will not know the difference but you will propel yourself toward burnout. You are not your client. Your client's growth is not a measure of your personal growth. The parameters need to be made clear and one of the ways to make them clear is to work with the client during the time that you are working with the client and let that be that. If supervision is necessary that is something else again, but that is something that is formally structured. When you leave your place of work, you leave it. You may have to fight your mind for a while in order to accomplish this, but it may be the difference of your remaining in the field and your getting burned out. Taking your work home with you does not make you a better counselor.

The discussion in a supervision group was on working with families who have had a family member commit suicide. As the discussion went on, one of the clinicians in the group looked more and more depressed. When I asked him what was going on with him he said, "The discussion is getting to me. This is a very serious problem area for me. I find that I take on my client's issues like lint and I am unable to pick them off. I know *how* to be different. I know the professional discipline that it takes. I know the principles of detachment. I know how to replace one thought with another. I know that I am not all-powerful and cannot fix everything for everybody. None of that knowledge seems to do me any good. What do you suppose this means?"

"It's certainly a boundary issue for you," I said. "Your parents never respected your boundaries. They constantly humiliated you in public. They took credit for that which you did that was good and wonderful. They never let you be separate from them. They never let you develop and separate yourself as a person. I suspect that this is a reason why you're going to be the opposite of your parents. You are so angry at your parents and so critical of your parents that whatever they say, whatever they do, however they behave there is a red flag saying I will behave the opposite. Since they were always angry, you never allow yourself to be angry. Since they were always out of control, you always need to maintain control.

"I suspect they also had no compassion for other human

beings. They certainly had no compassion or sensitivity towards what you were feeling and certainly did not spend time and demonstrate concern with what was going on with you. Here again you have decided to be the opposite of them. In so doing you have become over-involved. You are too caring."

It is the extremes with which we must concern ourselves. Because your parents were not caring does not mean that you need to be all-consumed with the caring. It does mean that you have to move a little bit more toward their position. The ideal for both you and your parents is to be more centered. The reality is that for your own growth, you need in some ways to be more like them.

CoA COUNSELORS HAVE A NEED FOR THEIR CLIENTS TO LIKE THEM. THEY SEEK APPROVAL NOT ONLY FROM THEIR SUPERVISORS AND PEERS BUT ALSO FROM THEIR CLIENTS.

This is another area that can become burdensome for you. Clients will simply not like you all of the time. It is part of your responsibility to do and say things that they do not like. They are not in a place to separate out your words from your person and they will get angry at you. This goes with the territory. You need to be very careful not to carry this response around with you. The important thing is that your client hears and does the things that are to his or her benefit. The important thing is the positive movement toward growth.

I had a client of mine call me from a rehab center. She was very angry with me. She said to me, "You told me I would not have a great deal of difficulty with withdrawal and I had a terrible time." My response was, "That was because I didn't realize how bad a shape you were in."

She began to laugh. I did not have to take on her anger. I did not have to defend myself. I was able to affect her getting the help that she requires. That is my job. That is my goal. If she needs someone to blame if she is angry, so be it. The blaming will not last long. It will stop when she begins to feel better. But her interests are my interests. It's very hard to separate that out if you are looking for your client's approval.

I suggest that if you need to seek approval — and we all do to one degree or another — you seek it from people who are in at least as good a shape as you are. If your clients are in at least as good shape as you are, you may want to reconsider what you are doing for a living.

ADULT CHILDREN OF ALCOHOLICS WHO ARE CLINICIANS AVOID CONFLICT.

It is certainly understandable that if you grew up in a home where there was always conflict and never resolution, you would back away from it. If you grew up in a home where you were afraid when anger was expressed that either you would be hurt or that someone else would be hurt or that you would be invisible or that someone else would be rejected, it is not difficult to see why you would discourage this kind of behavior.

It is a part of the therapeutic process for the client to learn to deal with his or her anger. It is a necessary part of the therapeutic process for you and your client to enter into conflict. If this does not happen, ever, you really need to take a hard look at what you are doing that prevents it from happening.

Another aspect that you have to look at critically is whether or not you yourself know how to resolve conflict. It may be absolutely essential not only in your own life but in your professional life that you develop the necessary tools to deal with working through and resolving conflict.

ADULT CHILDREN OF ALCOHOLICS HAVE DIFFICULTY MAKING REFERRALS.

The difficulty in making referrals comes from a fear of being found out. If you make a referral, the fear is that others will discover that you are incompetent. They will learn that you could not work with this client, and that you did not have the necessary skills to work with this client. You don't want people to know your limitations. The reality is that we all have limitations and the idea is not to try to hide them but to recognize them. In recognizing that there are others who are more skilled with certain clients than we are, we better serve our clients. We cannot be specialists in all areas. We cannot relate to *all* the people who come to see us. It is not possible nor is it desirable. "I cannot help you but I can help you find somebody who can" is a statement of competence.

CoA PROFESSIONALS HAVE IMPATIENCE WITH STUCK CLIENTS.

This results from self-judgment, in part, and a judgment of the client on the other part. The self-judgment is, "If I were a better clinician, my client would not get stuck. Therefore, the inability of my client to move at this time is a negative reflection on me."

The other part of it is a counter-transference issue with your client. "I was where you are and I got through it, I got by it, I did what I had to do. Why can't you?"

There may be two realities here. One may be that your client only looks stuck. Sometimes people need time in order to solidify their learnings. Sometimes people need to take a breather before they move on and make new decisions. Some-times, clients remain stuck so that they don't have to make the change which is so terrifying to them.

The other aspect is that there may be something you could be doing for your client that you are not doing. Believing that it is an inadequacy in you that causes your client to be stuck will get in the way of your asking a supervisor or a fellow counselor for some thoughts of what they would do if they were in this position.

"My client is stuck" and "I must fix" are not equivalent statements.

MANY LOOK FOR A TREATMENT ROAD MAP

Many want to know before they begin with a client just exactly what to do, how to take it, where to take it, how long it will take, what is the best approach to take, what one should not do, and so on. It's not unusual for one to get this request. Essentially it's asking for a road map through treatment. It's not a whole lot different from the road map that many CoAs want for their lives. "Tell me what to do. Tell me how to handle myself. Tell me if I am doing the right thing. Tell me if I am doing the wrong thing. Is this a good decision to make? Is this a

poor decision to make?" This difficulty and this need for structure, order, and direction is a legacy from childhood. Because
there was no foundation on which to build, there is a great
deal of insecurity left as to deciding what is the correct road to
take.

Those of us who train counselors would be disrespectful in
giving you a treatment road map. There is no treatment road
map just as there is no life road map. There are the things that
work and the things that don't work. There are the things that
one tests out that work successfully, and there are things that
one tests that don't work out so successfully. It is important to
be able to help your client discover options and alternatives, to
help your client be aware of the possible consequences of
exploring each one of these options and alternatives. If this is
what you are truly asking, if this is what you are truly looking
for, it is different from looking for a road map. It is saying,
"What are the different courses that this treatment could take?
What are the possibilities that I need to be mindful of before I
begin? What are my goals and what are my client's goals?"
Those are legitimate questions. Those are important questions.
Those questions may need to be asked.

ADULT CHILDREN OF ALCOHOLICS WHO ARE CLINICIANS ARE POOR STRESS MANAGERS.

Being stressed has been the natural order of things. You
grew up in a stress-filled household. It was what you knew. It
was the way that you felt all the time. As a result in the workplace when you are stressed, you are not necessarily aware of
it. Working with clients is very difficult. Working with clients is
a highly stressed situation. You do not have an opportunity to
relax; you do not have an opportunity to give anyone less than
your full attention. If you are relaxing or if you are giving your
client less than your full attention, you are not doing your job.
Therefore, by definition, you are in a highly stressed situation.
This isn't to say that it cannot be really satisfying. This is not to
say that this is not the way that you would prefer to work. What
it does say is that it is important for you to recognize that this
stress must be managed. It is important that you recognize that

you must take relief from the stress. It is important that you develop the means for doing so.

ADULT CHILDREN OF ALCOHOLICS WHO ARE CLINICIANS DENY THEIR OWN COUNTER-TRANSFERENCE.

Counter-transference somehow is a dirty word. Clinicians are not *supposed* to counter-transfer. Clients are *supposed* to transfer but clinicians are not *supposed* to counter-transfer. Therefore, a clinician who has a counter-transference reaction to a client is less than perfect. So since CoAs who are clinicians have to be perfect, they will tend to deny their own counter-transferance. It is not possible not to counter-transfer with at least some of your clients. It is not possible for you not to be drawn to a child that you would like to take home. It is not possible for you not to be furious at someone who behaves as someone in your life who abused you. It is not possible for you always not to be sexually drawn toward a client. This is simply the way that it is. Admitting it to yourself means that you can get a handle on it. Sometimes it's not serious. Sometimes your awareness of your response to this client means it will not get in your way.

Sometimes a reaction is so powerful that it becomes necessary for you to refer that client to somebody else. This is not a reflection on you. If it happens consistently, you may want to take a good hard look at it. It is not useful for you to deny it. The transference of the client to the counselor is a very useful one for the CoA. It is not harmful for the clinician to be proud of the client's growth and progress. This pride is certainly a parental pride. It feels good and it is not at all harmful to the client. If it goes much further than that, one needs to be careful. I know I had to stop seeing young children. My counter-transference reaction to them was too great. I wanted to bring all of them home with me. I wanted to take care of them. They had in fact become mine. This was not useful or beneficial to them, nor was it useful or beneficial to me.

CoAs WHO ARE CLINICIANS TEND TO NOT LIMIT THEIR CASELOADS.

You are the one in the agency who will take on that additional case. You are the one they can always be sure has space for one more. This has to do with your not knowing your own limitations. This has to do with your inability to say "no". This has to do with your not recognizing it when you are being exploited.

It is very important that you are careful to recognize just how many clients it is appropriate for you to handle and at what point it is a good idea for you to say "no". Check around. Don't do this necessarily within your own agency, because if you are being exploited there is a real good chance that others are being exploited too. Check around with people who work in other places and feel comfortable with their workload. See if they are carrying as many clients as you are. See how their case management is worked out. Where in your day is time built in for the paperwork that piles up way over your head? Where is time built in for you to return phone calls? This is all part of your job description. If you are seeing clients from the minute you walk in until the minute you leave and then have to do this work on your own, it is inappropriate, it is exploitive. Steps need to be taken to balance this out.

This may be a good opportunity to check yourself and find out if you are propelling towards burnout. The counselor who does not take careful precautions does not last in this field. Balance is the goal. All of these feelings are present some of the time, but on a scale of 1 to 5, any more than a 2 is the danger zone.

The Balance-Burnout Checklist for Counselors

Emotional Health

1. How much time do you spend worrying about your clients and their problems?
2. Are there moments when you believe that your work situation is hopeless and that you cannot help anyone?
3. Do you have strong mood swings and feelings about your clients? Your work? Your own family and friends?
4. How often do you blame your colleagues or your clients for your own bad feelings? The administration?
5. Would your life be fine if only staff and clients would behave differently?
6. How often do you feel lonely? When you're with others or by yourself?
7. Do you ever question your own sanity? Lose control?

8. When does your own behavior make you feel ashamed?
9. Are you often fearful?
10. Is work more important than your family and/or social life?
11. How do you control your anger and frustration?
12. What makes you feel responsible for the behavior of others?
13. Do you feel guilty about your work some of the time?
14. Do you feel overwhelmed by your working responsibilities?
15. Are you becoming more sensitive to and more critical of others at home and at work?

Physical Health

1. How are your sleeping habits being affected? Toss and turn? Escape by sleeping long hours?
2. What physical symptoms of illness in yourself have you noticed? Headaches? Nausea? "Knot" in the stomach? Exhaustion? Agitation? Backaches? Pains in the neck?
3. How have your eating habits changed?
4. Have you been involved in physical violence in your home or with friends?
5. How has your sexual life changed?

Social Health

1. How is your concentration on your work affecting your daily life? Working overtime? Not spending time with family and friends? Not taking time for recreation?
2. Do you spend much of your time reacting to crises and feeling your life is not your own?
3. Has life become so very serious that you have lost your sense of humor?
4. Do you find yourself forgetting things? Losing things? Having minor accidents?
5. Do you spend your free time during the working day talking about clients?
6. Do you have your clients check in with you regularly so that you may monitor their behavior?
7. How do you overprotect your clients?
8. What responsibilities have you given up in your family so that you may continue to concentrate on work?
9. How have you let work interfere with social plans?
10. Do you ever feel unappreciated at work?
11. Do you sometimes think your clients cannot survive without your good advice?
12. How do you let clients affect your own feelings? Your behavior?
13. Do you ever threaten clients or intimidate them in confrontations? Are you ever sarcastic?

Reprinted with permission from Hazelden: Manual for the Family Program for Professionals. Original concept by Terry Williams & Ruth Friedman.

Chapter Thirteen

THOUGHTS FOR EMPLOYEE ASSISTANCE PROGRAMS

An Employee Assistance Program is an ideal route to draw ACoAs into the treatment they need. Because people spend a large portion of their lives in the workplace, it is here, surrounded by colleagues who do not necessarily have the personal investment in the working relationship, that ACoA behavior can be perceived and addressed — for the good of both the individual and the company. There are no losers when the ACoA gets the care he or she needs and deserves.

For the individual, it can often serve as the deterrent from progressing into alcoholism or other forms of substance abuse, as Cindy tells us:

Five years ago, frightened by my own increased drinking, worried about the impact of alcoholism on another generation and supported by my own therapy, I made a decision to stop drinking and to face the personal and family problems related to multi-generational alcoholism which I had avoided and denied. The decision to take charge of my life and then to fulfill the Serenity Prayer has increasingly contributed to an understanding of my motivations and therefore a lessening of the necessity for me to work out my unresolved conflicts through the work itself . . .

It can help to quiet what Mark called "the inner voice of failure" that sabotages the personal as well as the professional life.

Michael, the manager of an EAP for a large high-tech research company, describes the benefits for the company as well as for the individual.

In almost every case they respond well to counseling . . . The degree of isolation, support systems, etc., determine the length of treatment. The prognosis for these clients is excellent once they are treated.

In other words, when you begin to address the issues of the ACoA in the workplace, you begin to address the **$190.7 billion** lost in 1980, according to work done by the Research Triangle Institute for the Alcohol, Drug Abuse and Mental Health Administration — money lost through lost sales, poor job performance, on-the-job accidents, absence from work, medical costs, and the costs of hiring and training new personnel.

But it was the religious counselor who most poignantly described the benefits of ACoA treatment:

God made you. It's OK to be you. It's even OK to love yourself. In fact, the more you can love yourself, the easier it is for you to help others.

This ideal exists in all relationships. It is a workplace goal as well as a personal goal. It is a direction for us all to follow.

Some companies are in a position to offer an educational series to their employees. The components of an educational series on and for adult children of alcoholics could be the following.

Week One: An Overview — Adult Children of Alcoholics

The first week is designed to include general information pertaining to ACoAs. This seminar introduces the education series and describes the content and focus of the seven following weeks.

OBJECTIVES:

Participants will learn of the cost of alcoholism and related problems to their company.

Participants will become familiar with the research, literature and experiences of the largest population of people affected by alcoholism.

Participants may identify themselves as belonging to this population.

Participants will have opportunity to ask questions and receive clarification on individual problems and concerns, and assess whether the education will be of further help.

Week Two: The Childhood Experience

This seminar introduces the "family disease" concept. The interpersonal dynamics of the alcoholic family are explained. The leader discusses early perceptions of reality and the coping mechanisms CoAs developed for survival.

OBJECTIVES:

Participants will become aware of the progressive processes of the family disease.

Participants will become aware of how these family dynamics can be replayed in the workplace.

Participants become familiarized with how a functional family system deals with problem solving, expression of emotions, and communication.

Week Three: Adaptation to Alcoholism

This seminar focuses on the roles assumed by family members, and how these roles are both functional and dysfunctional in childhood and adulthood. This lecture stresses the need for ACoAs to identify how roles serve as a protective defense from emotional turmoil as well as provide the ACoA with a sense of self based on what they do versus who they are and how they feel. This seminar includes a discussion on conditional versus unconditional love.

OBJECTIVES:

Participants will become familiarized with various roles assumed in alcoholic families and identify how various roles serve in maintaining survival, reducing stress, and create a sense of stability for the CoA.

Participants will discuss the strengths and weaknesses implied in various roles, what the advantages and disadvantages were, and what emotions the roles repressed.

Participants identify how the alcoholic and co-dependent parents responded conditionally to various role behaviors versus responding unconditionally to the whole child.

Week Four: Adult Traits and Characteristics

Discussion of adult traits and characteristics as determined by researchers. This seminar focuses on problems experienced by ACoAs and how these problems have roots in the family history of alcoholism. The messages and distorted perceptions internalized throughout childhood in an alcoholic environment are examined.

OBJECTIVES:

Participants will become aware of the manifestations of the employee's isolation in the workplace.

Participants will learn how these internalized overt or covert messages interfere with employee's present functioning.

Participants will develop strategies toward change.

Week Five: Self Help for ACoAs

This seminar uses a broad based definition of self help to assist the ACoA in utilizing resources to aid in recovery. The traditional programs of self-help such as A.A., Al-Anon and A.C.o.A. are discussed. The participants are also exposed to the help available through education and various community resources. Various forms of therapy are discussed.

OBJECTIVES:

Participants will become aware of the available recovery programs.

Participants will utilize a variety of resources to help with various needs.

Week Six: Intimacy

This seminar will, through lecture, film, discussion and group exercises, show how living with alcoholism can interfere with the ability to experience intimacy. The goal of this seminar is to define intimacy and discuss the components of healthy relationships.

OBJECTIVES:

Participants will discover how problems of intimacy can affect workplace behavior.

Week Seven: The Recovery Process

The seminar focuses on the recovery process as outlined by Gravitz and Bowden. Needs and problems encountered during various stages of recovery are discussed. The behavioral, cognitive and emotional changes experienced in recovery, and how change occurs is highlighted.

OBJECTIVES:

Understanding recovery as a process.

ACoA WARNING SIGNS: A Checklist for EAPs

Just as it takes time to get to know someone, it takes time to perceive the effects of an undiagnosed CoA on the job. Here are some of the most important manifestations of CoAs acting out on the job:

- Procrastination
- Perfectionism
- Indecisiveness
- Impulsiveness in decision-making
- Inconsistent productivity
- Too many questions
- No questions at all
- Difficulty in accepting compliments
- Constant approval-seeking
- Often working very late
- High absenteeism
- Overinvolvement with other employees' personal problems
- Apparent disregard for other employees' feelings
- Assuming responsibility for other people's mistakes
- Lack of initiative
- Frequent emotional outbursts
- No display of emotions at all
- Too much discussion of personal life
- No apparent life outside of work

The reader will see that many of the items on this list form pairs. The ACoA will often flip-flop from one extreme to the other — productivity is a case in point.

But it's important to note that these vary, depending on the nature of the workplace, and that this list is incomplete. Further research is required to determine whether CoAs create stress on the job, how they respond to it when it does occur, and what effect this has on their fellow employees.

CRISIS COUNSELING FOR ACoAs:

A Checklist for EAPs

1) Referred for job performance problems.
   Look first for signs of substance abuse.
2) Absenteeism due to illness.
   Check for burnout or substance abuse.
3) Problems with peers and supervisors.
   Look for playing out of alcohol family system.
4) Problems with family.
   Look for substance abuse or other compulsive behaviors in self, spouse or children.
   Look for lack of understanding of how to solve the problem.
5) Problems with intimacy.
   Look for fears of abandonment.
   Look for substance abuse in lover.
   Look for lover within the organization and the relationship going bad.

Chapter Fourteen

CONCLUSION

The legacy of childhood clearly demonstrates itself in the workplace. It is true for everyone regardless of their background. One's history can either work for them or against them. One can decide to change or adapt. Choices exist once there is insight.

Clinical practice clearly shows that CoAs respond very quickly to treatment. They are eager for help and make very good use of tools gained in the counseling process.

In the substance abuse field, we talk in terms of prevention, intervention and treatment.

Prevention lies in education. "I feel this way because of part of my childhood experience. I behave this way because of part of my childhood experience."

Intervention lies in breaking the cycle. "I need to make changes because what I'm doing and feeling is not working for me."

Treatment is the development of new messages.

I am a person of worth.

I can demonstrate it.

I can feel it.

I can make choices.

I can work for you and not lose me.

I can grow with the organization and not leave me behind.

I will take me with me.

The EAP counselor who works with the CoA participates in an exciting growth process. The shift from me (the object) to I (the subject) creates an energy that can be productive for all concerned.

The value of the CoA in the workplace gets clearer and clearer. Recognition of the signs of CoA issues as they surface, and responding quickly and appropriately to them will, in both the long and short run, result in maintaining superior workers and greatly reduce the losses due to burnout, physical problems, substance abuse and impulsive job changes. It is in the economic best interest of companies to be responsive. It is to the advantage of all — not just CoAs, but their colleagues as well — to address these issues as they arise, and not wait until they reach bitter fruition. The workplace itself will become a more productive and healthier environment.

APPENDIX:
RESEARCH DATA AND FINDINGS

In order to validate clinical research findings, it is important to discover if the data collected from a larger, random sample is consistent with the attitudes and feelings expressed by the clinical population.

The problems and how they manifest themselves have been discussed in the text. The corroborating evidence should prompt consideration of the cost-effectiveness for EAPs to provide appropriate intervention.

The study that follows is a very simple design. It is a self-reported questionnaire. The experimental group consisted of those who reported a parent or grandparent as alcoholic. The control group reported no alcoholism in their family.

Hypothesis
Individuals who grow up with alcoholism and those who do not feel differently about themselves in the workplace.

Experimental Group Findings
I. CoAs are represented in all job categories. The numbers are skewed, however, toward occupations that are usually considered stressful. These include: Counselor, Secretary, Nurse, Small Business Owner, Administrator, Sales Representative.

Further study is indicated to determine:
   a) Whether within given occupations, such as nursing, there are statistically higher numbers of CoAs.
   b) Whether within low-stress occupations CoAs create crisis and manufacture stress.
II. Our survey found that:
   a) 30% of the sample indicated feelings of inadequacy as their most predominant feeling on the job. This was significantly greater than any other feeling, and was not restricted to any single job category, age group or sex.

b) 10% of the sample indicated feelings of anger as their most predominant feeling on the job. This was not limited to any job category or sex but seemed to be expressed more by the older age groups.

c) 6% and 5% of those interviewed said that lack of control and being unappreciated were their predominant feelings on the job.

III. The seven most predominant feelings for men were:
— Inadequacy
— Anger
— Lack of recognition
— Fear of rejection
— Lack of control
— Boredom
— Perfection

The seven most predominant feelings for women were:
— Inadequacy
— Anger
— Lack of control
— Lack of appreciation
— Frustration
— Boredom
— Perfection

The study also found, in regards to predominant feelings, that:

- Feelings of inadequacy ranked first for both groups.
- Feelings of anger ranked second for both groups.
- Lack of control, boredom, and perfectionism were among the top seven for both groups.
- Men included lack of recognition and fear of rejection.
- Women included lack of appreciation and frustration.

IV. Scores from CoAs who are in recovery from alcoholism were looked at separately to determine if they had different reactions than the non-recovering CoAs. The feelings ran the entire spectrum, indicating that those ACoAs in recovery and those who were not were similar. This suggests that recovery from alcoholism is different from overcoming the experience of growing up with alcoholism and should be looked at separately. The dynamics of alcoholism and addiction may compound the issues but should be considered as having their own symptomology and treatment.

The only meaningful difference between those who were in recovery from alcoholism and those who were not showed up when a comparison was made of the two most prominent self-feelings — inadequacy and anger.

Of the number who reported that they were either recovering or not alcoholics:

	Non-alcoholic	Alcoholic
Feelings of Inadequacy	26/56 (46%)	14/46 (30%)
Feelings of Anger	6/56 (11%)	11/46 (24%)

Feelings of inadequacy do not mask other feelings; on the other hand, feelings of anger may cover up deeper feelings. Whether or not the anger is a cover-up for feelings of inadequacy is worth pursuing clinically. Certainly, the up-front feelings of anger manifest differently from the up-front feelings of inadequacy.

As a result, the consequences may vary and the problems that come to the attention of EAP counselors may be different. But the clinical intervention, if it is to address more than behavior modification, may be similar.

Control Group Findings

I. The largest number of respondents in the control group did not answer the question, "What is the bad feeling you have had most often on the job?" (22%). When queried by the researcher, the responses were ambivalent.

II. The second largest number responded that they had no bad feelings on the job. (13%)

III. Those two groups combined were a total of 35% of the controls.

   This indicates either a general lack of awareness or denial

on the part of the respondents. Even if there are no major job complaints, the question is stated in such a way that the condition does not have to be constant, pervasive, or overwhelming.

IV. The next largest number (12%) reported stress as the most predominant bad feeling in the workplace.

This was equal with men and women.

Comparison of Experimental and Control Groups

I. All of the CoAs reported a predominant bad feeling as compared to the large number in the control group who either stated that the question did not apply or that they had no bad feeling.

II. Stress as the most reported bad feeling shows a major difference between the experimental and control groups. CoAs enjoy the experience of stress, the familiarity of the feeling and ignore the warning signs.

III. Only 3% of the control group, as opposed to 30% of the experimental group, reported inadequacy as the primary bad feeling. The difference in self-confidence is an important factor. (The fact that only women in the control group reported this feeling is suggestive.)

IV. Although a few of the control group reported frustration as their predominant feeling, none reported anger, the second most predominant feeling for the experimental group. The difference in the degree of the reaction between the two groups may be a relevant factor.

V. The large numbers in the control group who denied the relevance of the question about bad feelings, as opposed to the 100% response to the question by CoAs, suggests that either the CoAs are more tuned in to their feelings or that their feelings are too strong to be denied.

The hypothesis that there are differences in the feelings in the workplace between ACoAs and those from other family systems is sustained.

The premise of this book — that this group is identifiable and can be intervened upon and serviced in the workplace would appear to be supported by the evidence.

Research Procedure

A questionnaire was drafted with the following requested information:

Sex

Age

Address (City, State)

Profession, Job Description and Salary Range

Bad Feeling most often on Job

What Family Role was played?

The questionnaires were distributed to 248 ACoAs and a control group of 117 respondents.

Occupations

Table 3-3 summarizes the resultant occupational grouping of the ACoAs surveyed and Figure 3-5, 3-6 and 3-7 graphically depict the relationships of the occupations for each sex.

Figure 3-5 delineates the occupations in which 4 or more ACoAs were engaged (this included 165 ACoAs) — 73 ACoAs were engaged in an occupation which included 3 or less ACoAs, 1 ACoA was unemployed, 1 ACoA was disabled and 1 ACoA did not reply.

Figure 3-6 delineates the occupations in which 3 or more ACoAs were engaged. (This included 33 male ACoAs) — 31 male ACoAs were engaged in an occupation which included 2 or 1 male ACoA, and 1 male ACoAs was unemployed.

Figure 3-7 delineates the occupation in which 3 or more female ACoAs were engaged. (This included 127 female ACoAs) — 47 female ACoAs were engaged in an occupation which included 2 or 1 female ACoAs, 1 female ACoA was disabled and 1 female ACoA did not reply.

ACoA Research Questionnaire

Sex: M_____ F_____   Age: 20_____30 31_____40 41_____50 51 and over_____

Address (City and State only) _____

Alcoholic: Yes_____ No_____

Do/did you have a parent or grandparent who abused alcohol
or drugs? Yes_____ No_____

Do/did you have a brother, sister, or child who abused alcohol
or drugs? Yes_____ No_____

Do/did you live with chronic illness? Yes_____ No_____

Were you adopted? Yes_____ No_____

Were you in foster care? Yes_____ No_____

Were you physically or emotionally abused? Yes_____ No_____

Was your family profoundly religious? Yes_____ No_____

Were you an "Army Brat"? Yes_____ No_____

Profession:_____ Job Description: _____

Salary Range:	$10,000 to $20,000 _____	$21,000 to $30,000 _____	$31,000 to $40,000 _____	Over $40,000 _____

What is the bad feeling you have **most often** on the job? _____

What role did you have in your family of origin? _____

TABLES AND FIGURES

Table 3-1 summarizes the resultant sex grouping of the ACoAs surveyed and Figure 3-1 depicts graphically the percentage relationship between the number of females and the number of males surveyed.

TABLE 3-1
SEX GROUPING

Number of Males	Number of Females	Incomplete Questionnaires	Total
65	176	7	248

FIGURE 3-1
SEX GROUPING — PERCENTAGE
(Based on 241 Total ACoAs)

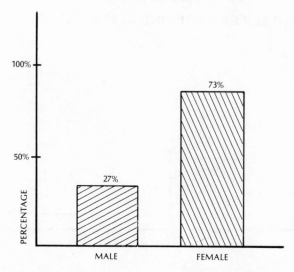

As the Table and Figure show, a total of 248 ACoAs were surveyed with 176 being female and 65 being male (approximately a 3:1 ratio) — 7 did not complete the sex portion of the questionnaire.

3-2 AGE

Table 3-2 summarizes the resultant sex grouping of the ACoAs surveyed and Figures 3-2, 3-3 and 3-4 depict graphically the percentage relationships between the age groups for each sex.

TABLE 3-2
AGE GROUPING

AGE (YRS)	NUMBER OF MALES	NUMBER OF FEMALES	TOTAL
20-30	13	39	52
31-40	23	91	114
41-50	23	33	56
51+	6	13	19
TOTAL	65	176	241

FIGURE 3-2
TOTAL AGE GROUPING — PERCENTAGE
(Based on 241 ACoAs)

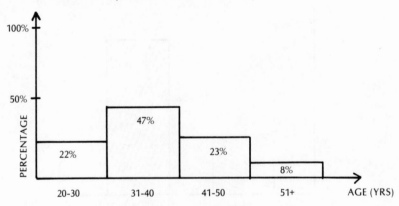

It is noted from the Table and the Figures that the dominant female age group surveyed was the 31-40 group (52% of the females) while the dominant male age groups surveyed were the 31-40 and 41-50 age groups (35% each of the males).

FIGURE 3-3

FEMALE AGE GROUPING — PERCENTAGE

(Based on 176 Females)

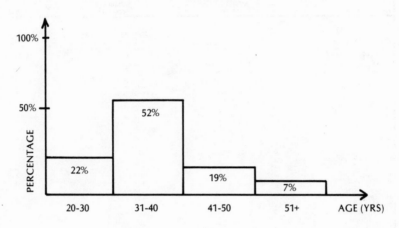

FIGURE 3-4

MALE AGE GROUPING — PERCENTAGE

(Based on 65 Males)

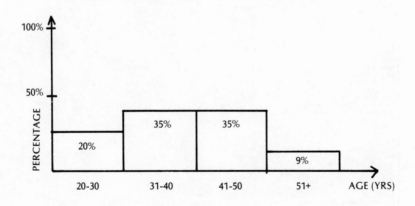

———————————TABLE 3-3 ———————————

OCCUPATION — SEX — AGE GROUPING

Note: (2-3), (3-4), (4-5), and (5+) Denote the Respective Age Groups of (21-30), (31-40), (41-50) and (51+)

OCCUPATION		NUMBER OF MALES	NUMBER OF FEMALES	TOTAL
Counselor	(135)	3-(3);-3	3-(2), 4-(3), 5-(4), 2-(5);-14	17
Secretary	(26)	0	2-(2), 5-(3), 3-(4), 2-(5);-12	12
Registered Nurse	(27)	0	2-(2), 6-(3), 3-(4);-11	11
Small Business Owner	(133)	1-(2), 2-(3), 3-(4), 1-(5);-7	1-(2), 1-(4), 1-(5);-3	10
Administrator	(998)	0	3-(2), 6-(3), 1-(5);-12	10
Sales Representative	(48)	1-(3), 1-(4), 3-(5);-5	2-(2), 2-(4), 1-(5);-5	10
Teacher	(47)	1-(4), 1-(5);-2	1-(2), 6-(3);-7	9
Homemaker	(142)	0	5-(3), 2-(4), 2-(5);-9	9
Clerical Worker	(39)	0	3-(2), 3-(3), 2-(4);-8	8
Accountant	(77)	2-(2), 1-(3);-3	2-(2), 1-(3), 2-(4);-5	8
Manager	(99A)	1-(2), 3-(3);-4	2-(3), 1-(4), 1-(5);-4	8
Social Worker	(24)	0	1-(2), 6-(3);-7	7
Student	(130)	4-(2);-4	2-(2);-2	6
Self Employed	(136)	1-(3), 1-(5);-2	1-(2), 3-(3);-4	6
Health Technician	(1)	0	2-(2), 2-(3), 1-(4);-5	5
Commercial Writer	(138)	1-(4);-1	2-(2), 1-(3), 1-(5);-4	5
Bookkeeper	(56)	0	1-(2), 1-(3), 1-(4), 1-(5);-4	4
Engineer	(61)	2-(2), 1-(3), 1-(4);-4	0	4
Librarian	(68)	0	4-(3);-4	4
Lawyer	(86)	0	2-(2), 1-(3), 1-(4);-4	4
Bus Driver	(91)	2-(3);-2	2-(4);-2	4
Credit Rep/Mgr	(156)	0	4-(3);-4	4
Research Worker	(14)	0	3-(2);-3	3
Hair Dresser	(18)	1-(3);-1	1-(3), 1-(4);-2	3
Mechanic	(38)	3-(4);-3	0	3
College Personnel	(92)	1-(4);-1	1-(2), 1-(3);-2	3
Practical Nurse	(3)	0	1-(2), 1-(3);-2	2
Sales Manager	(34)	2-(4);-2	0	2
Clergy	(36)	1-(4);-1	1-(4);-1	2
Construction	(50)	2-(4);-2	0	2
Insurance Agent	(63)	2-(4);-2	0	2
Policeman	(70)	1-(4);-1	1-(3);-1	2
Personnel	(117)	0	1-(2), 1-(3);-2	2
Technician	(134)	2-(3);-2	0	2
Retail	(146)	1-(2), 1-(3);-2	0	2
Legal Assistant	(149)	0	2-(3);-2	2
Travel	(151)	0	2-(3);-2	2
Flight Attendant	(160)	0	2-(3);-2	2
Waitress	(2)	0	1-(2);-1	1
Dental Assistants	(12)	0	1-(3);-1	1
Computer Programmer	(15)	0	1-(3);-1	1
Artist	(19)	1-(4);-1	0	1
Health Aid	(20)	0	1-(3);-1	1
Taxi Driver	(21)	1-(3);-1	0	1
Chemist	(22)	0	1-(3);-1	1
Insurance Adjuster	(42)	0	1-(3);-1	1
Office Manager	(45)	0	1-(4);-1	1
Editor	(46)	0	1-(4);-1	1
Janitor	(78)	1-(3);-1	0	1
Truck Driver	(80)	1-(4);-1	0	1
Fireman	(82)	1-(3);-1	0	1
Bank Financial Manager	(85)	1-(4);-1	0	1
Child Care Worker	(87)	0	1-(3);-1	1
Electric Technician	(96)	0	1-(3);-1	1
Physician	(106)	0	1-(3);-1	1
Sonic Welder Supervisor	(131)	1-(2);-1	0	1
Small Grocery-Does Everything	(132)	1-(2);-1	0	1
Economist	(137)	1-(3);-1	0	1
Pilot	(139)	1-(4);-1	0	1
Bartender	(140)	0	1-(2);-1	1
Cosmetologist	(141)	0	1-(2);-1	1
Psychiatrist	(143)	0	1-(3);-1	1
Psychotherapist	(144)	0	1-(3);-1	1
Psychologist	(145)	0	1-(3);-1	1
Senior Program Analyst	(147)	0	1-(4);-1	1
Radio News Reporter	(148)	0	1-(3);-1	1
Probation Officer	(150)	0	1-(3);-1	1
Photo Retoucher	(152)	0	1-(3);-1	1
Broker Lease	(153)	0	1-(5);-1	1
Continuity Director-TV	(154)	0	1-(4);-1	1
Receptionist	(155)	0	1-(3);-1	1
Wardrobe Consultant	(157)	0	1-(3);-1	1
Computer/Dp Project Mgr	(152)	0	1-(3);-1	1
Cashier	(159)	0	1-(3);-1	1
Senior Court Deputy	(161)	0	1-(4);-1	1

UE — 1M(3), D.A. — 1F(4); NO REPLY — 1F(3)   64   174   238

_____ **FIGURE 3-5** _____

ACoA OCCUPATIONAL GROUPING (238 ACoAs)
(4 or more ACoAs in an occupation: Total of 165 ACoAs or 69%)

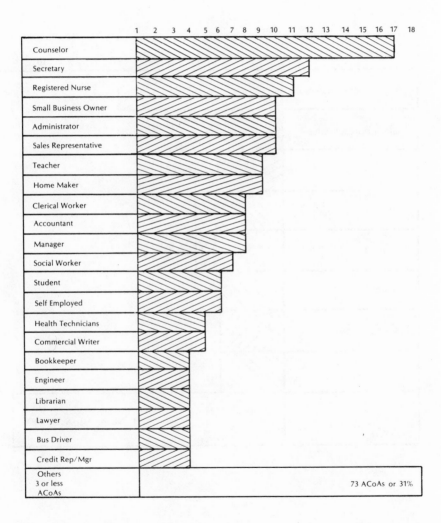

─────────── **FIGURE 3-6** ───────────

MALE ACoA OCCUPATIONAL GROUPING (64 MALE ACoAs)
(3 or more male ACoAs in an occupation: Total of 33 or 52%)

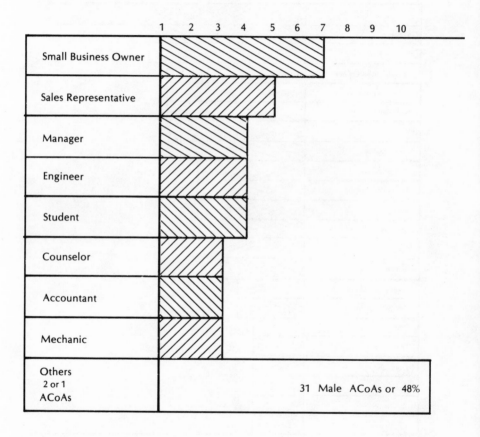

FIGURE 3-7

FEMALE ACoA OCCUPATIONAL GROUPING
(174 ACoAs)
(3 or more female ACoAs in an occupation: Total of 127 or 73%)

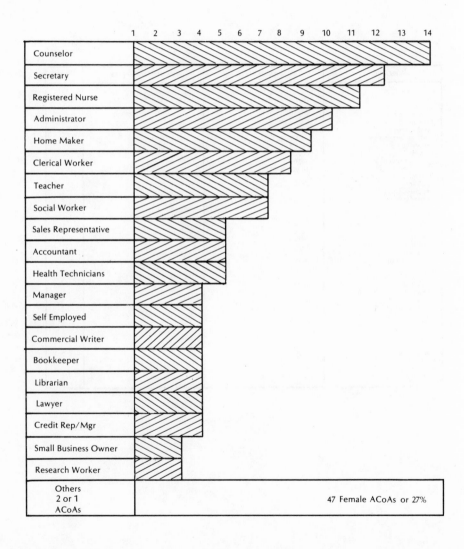

TABLE 3-4

FEELINGS — SEX — AGE GROUPING

FEELING	NUMBER OF MALES	NUMBER OF FEMALES	TOTAL
Inadequacy	5-(2), 7-(3), 3-(4), 1-(5);-16	13-(2), 29-(3), 12-(4), 2-(5);-56	72
Anger	2-(3), 4-(4), 1-(5);-7	2-(2), 7-(3), 7-(4), 2-(5);-18	25
Lack of Control	2-(2), 1-(5);-3	3-(2), 9-(3);-12	15
Unappreciated	1-(2);1	1-(2), 7-(3), 1-(4), 1-(5);-10	11
Bored	1-(2), 2-(3);-3	4-(2), 1-(3), 1-(5);-6	9
Perfectionism	3-(3);-3	1-(2), 3-(3), 2-(5);-6	9
Lack of Recognition	1-(3), 3-(4), 1-(5);-5	1-(2), 3-(3);-4	9
Frustration	1-(3), 1-(4);-2	1-(2), 5-(3), 1-(4);-7	9
Fear of Rejection	2-(2), 1-(3), 1-(5);-4	3-(3);-3	7
Low Self Esteem/Worth	1-(3);-1	2-(2), 2-(3);-4	5
Fear of Authority	1-(3), 1-(4);-2	2-(2), 1-(3);-3	5
Fear of Failure	0	3-(2), 2-(3);-5	5
Isolation	0	3-(3), 1-(4), 1-(5);-5	5
Approval Seeking	2-	1-(2), 1-(3);-2	4
Abandonment	1-(4), 1-(5);-2	1-(3);-1	3
Burnout	0	1-(2), 1-(3);-2	2
Over Responsible	0	1-(2), 1-(3);-2	2
Confused	1-(2);-1	1-(2);-1	2
Helpless	0	2-(3);-2	2
Loneliness	2-(4);-2	0	2
Fear of Success	1-(3);-1	1-(3);-1	2
Anxiety	0	1-(3), 1-(4);-2	2
Feeling Inferior	0	2-(5);-2	2
Lack of Respect	0	1-(2);-1	1
Need to Rescue	0	1-(3);-1	1
Intimidated	1-(3);-1	0	1
Unable to Communicate	1-(4);-1	0	1
Lack of Ambition	0	1-(3);-1	1
Feeling Victimized	0	1-(3);-1	1
Misunderstood	0	1-(3);-1	1
Stressful	0	1-(3);-1	1
Unproductive	0	1-(4);-1	1
Powerless	0	1-(4);-1	1
Indecisive	0	1-(5);-1	1
Being Different	1-(4);-1		1
Satisfied	1-(4);-1		1
Grandiose	1-(4);-1		1
No Reply	1-(3),-1	2-(3), 2-(4);-4	5

FIGURE 3-8

TOTAL ACoA FEELINGS GROUPING (236)*
(Feelings expressed by 3 or more ACoAs: 206 ACoAs or 87%)

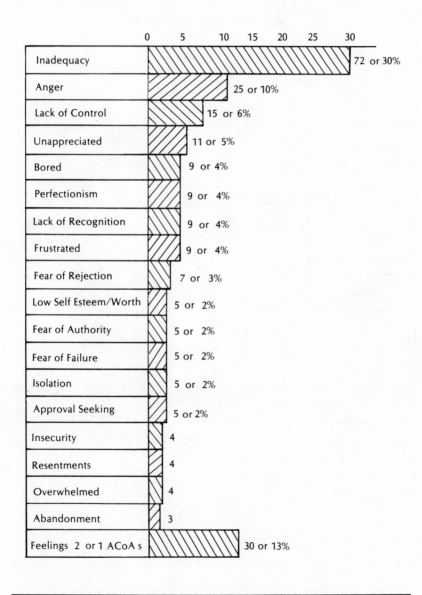

Inadequacy	72 or 30%
Anger	25 or 10%
Lack of Control	15 or 6%
Unappreciated	11 or 5%
Bored	9 or 4%
Perfectionism	9 or 4%
Lack of Recognition	9 or 4%
Frustrated	9 or 4%
Fear of Rejection	7 or 3%
Low Self Esteem/Worth	5 or 2%
Fear of Authority	5 or 2%
Fear of Failure	5 or 2%
Isolation	5 or 2%
Approval Seeking	5 or 2%
Insecurity	4
Resentments	4
Overwhelmed	4
Abandonment	3
Feelings 2 or 1 ACoA s	30 or 13%

FIGURE 3-9

MALE ACoA FEELINGS GROUPING (64)*
(Feelings Expressed by 3 or More Male ACoAs:
41 Male ACoAs or 64%)

NUMBER OF MALE ACoAs

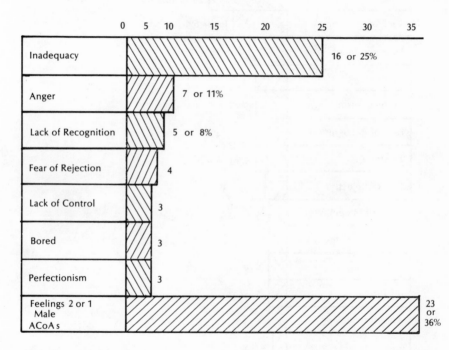

* 1 had no reply

FIGURE 3-10

FEMALE ACoA FEELINGS GROUPING (172)*
(Feelings Expressed by 3 or More Female ACoAs:
146 Females or 85%)

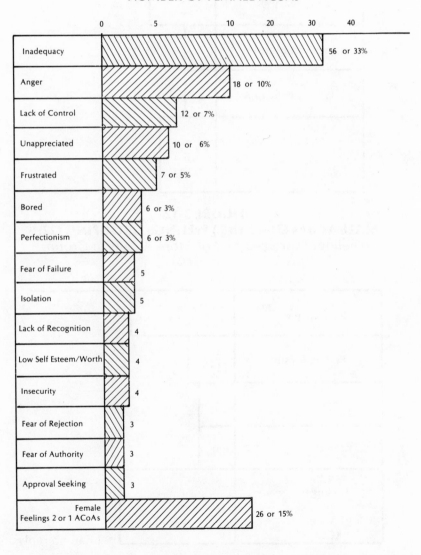

NUMBER OF FEMALE ACoAs

FIGURE 3-11

MALE ACoAs (20-30 YRS.) FEELINGS GROUPING (13)
(Feelings Expressed by 2 or More ACoAs in Group:
9 or 69%)

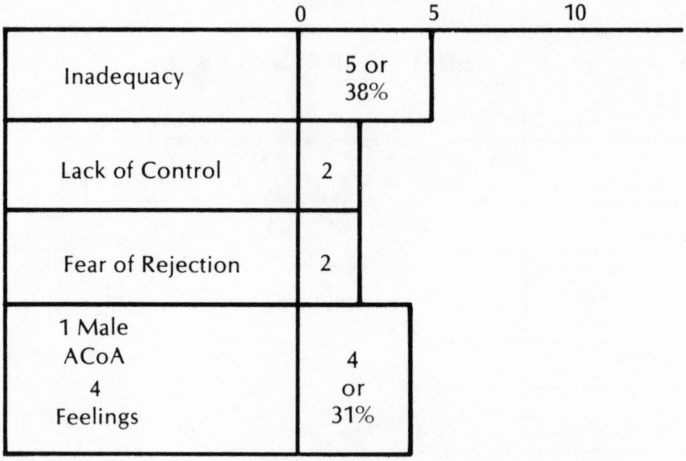

	0	5	10
Inadequacy	5 or 38%		
Lack of Control	2		
Fear of Rejection	2		
1 Male ACoA 4 Feelings	4 or 31%		

FIGURE 3-12

MALE ACoAs (31-40 YRS.) FEELINGS GROUPING (22)*
(Feelings Expressed by 2 or More ACoAs in Group:
14 or 64%)

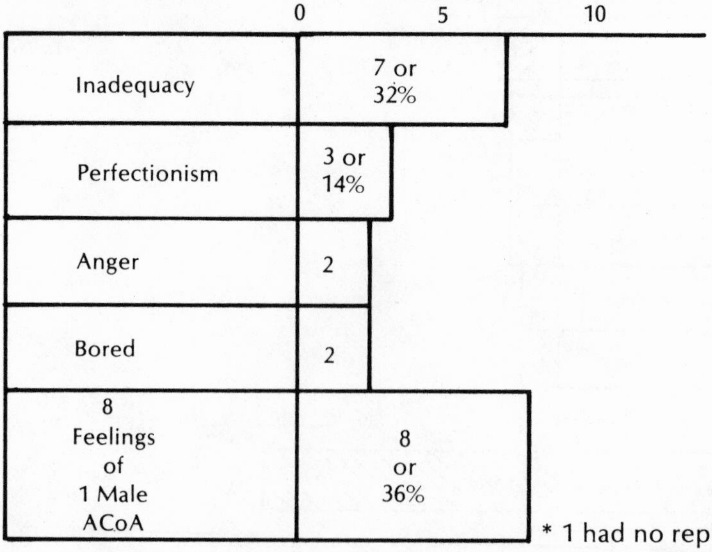

	0	5	10
Inadequacy	7 or 32%		
Perfectionism	3 or 14%		
Anger	2		
Bored	2		
8 Feelings of 1 Male ACoA	8 or 36%		

* 1 had no reply

---------------------------**FIGURE 3-13**---------------------------

MALE ACoAs (41-50 YRS.) FEELINGS GROUPING (23)
(Feelings Expressed by 2 or More ACoAs in Group:
14 or 61%)

	0	5	10
Anger	4 or 17%		
Inadequacy	3 or 13%		
Lack of Recognition	3 or 13%		
Approval Seeking	2		
Loneliness	2		
9 Feelings of 1 Male ACoA			9 or 39%

NOTE:

Each of the 6 male ACoAs over 51 expressed 6 different feelings — therefore, no age-feeling correlation.

---------------------FIGURE 3-14---------------------

FEMALE ACoAs (20-30 YRS.) Feelings Grouping (39)
*(Feelings Expressed by 2 or More ACoAs in Group:
29 or 74%)*

NUMBER OF FEMALE ACoAs

	0	2	4	6	8	10	12	14

Inadequacy	13 or 33%
Bored	4 or 10%
Lack of Control	3
Fear of Failure	3
Anger	2
Low Self Esteem/Worth	2
Fear of Authority	2
1 Female ACoA 10 Feelings	10 or 30%

—————————— FIGURE 3-15 ——————————

FEMALE ACoAs (31-40 YRS.) FEELINGS GROUPING (89)*
(Feelings Expressed by 2 or More ACoAs in Group:
75 or 84%)

	0 2 4 6 8 10 12 14 16 18 20 22 24 26 28 30
Inadequacy	29 or 33%
Lack of Control	9 or 13%
Anger	7 or 8%
Unappreciated	7 or 8%
Frustrated	5 or 6%
Perfectionism	3
Lack of Recognition	3
Fear of Rejection	3
Isolation	3
Low Self Esteem/Worth	2
Fear of Failure	2
Helpless	2
1 Female 14 ACoA Feelings	14 or 16%

* 2 had no reply

——————————— **FIGURE 3-16** ———————————

FEMALE ACoAs (41-50 YRS.) FEELINGS GROUPING (31)*
*(Feelings Expressed by 2 or More ACoAs in Group:
23 or 74%)*

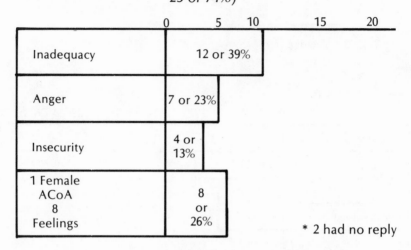

	0	5	10	15	20
Inadequacy	12 or 39%				
Anger	7 or 23%				
Insecurity	4 or 13%				
1 Female ACoA 8 Feelings	8 or 26%				

* 2 had no reply

FIGURE 3-17
FEMALE ACoAs (51 + YRS.) FEELINGS GROUPING (13)
*(Feelings Expressed by 2 or More ACoAs in Group:
8 or 62%)*

	0	5	10	15
Inadequacy	2			
Anger	2			
Perfectionism	2			
Feeling Inferior	2			
1 Female ACoA 5 Feelings	5 or 38%			

———————————— **FIGURE 3-18**————————————

ALL ACoAs (20-30 YRS.) FEELINGS GROUPING (52)
(Feelings Expressed by 3 or More ACoAs in Age Group:
31 or 60%)

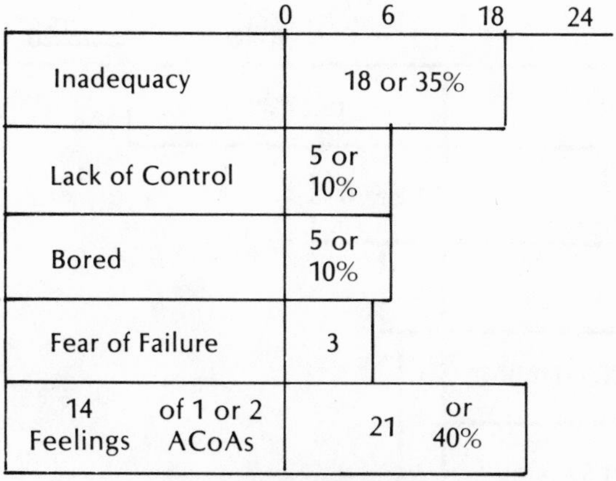

	0	6	18	24
Inadequacy		18 or 35%		
Lack of Control		5 or 10%		
Bored		5 or 10%		
Fear of Failure	3			
14 of 1 or 2 Feelings ACoAs		21 or 40%		

FIGURE 3-19
ALL ACoAs (31-40 YRS.) FEELINGS GROUPING (111)*
(Feelings Expressed by 3 or More ACoAs in Age Group:
90 or 81%)

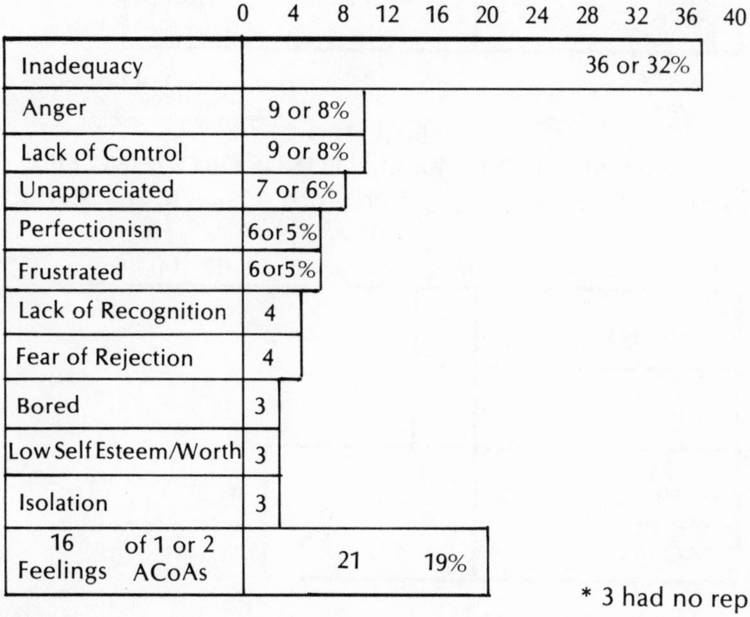

	0	4	8	12	16	20	24	28	32	36	40
Inadequacy									36 or 32%		
Anger	9 or 8%										
Lack of Control	9 or 8%										
Unappreciated	7 or 6%										
Perfectionism	6 or 5%										
Frustrated	6 or 5%										
Lack of Recognition	4										
Fear of Rejection	4										
Bored	3										
Low Self Esteem/Worth	3										
Isolation	3										
16 of 1 or 2 Feelings ACoAs		21 19%									

* 3 had no reply

———————————————— **FIGURE 3-20** ————————————————

ALL ACoAs (41-50 YRS.) FEELINGS GROUPING (54)*
(Feelings Expressed by 3 or More ACoAs in Age Group:
36 or 67%)

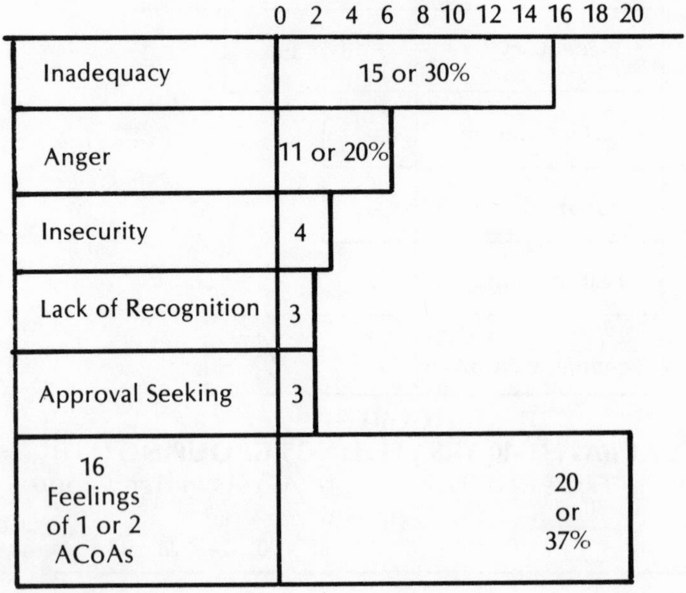

0 2 4 6 8 10 12 14 16 18 20

Inadequacy	15 or 30%
Anger	11 or 20%
Insecurity	4
Lack of Recognition	3
Approval Seeking	3
16 Feelings of 1 or 2 ACoAs	20 or 37%

* 2 had no reply

FIGURE 3-21
ALL ACoAs (51 + YRS.) FEELINGS GROUPING (19)
(Feelings Expressed by 3 or More ACoAs in Age Group:
6 or 32%)

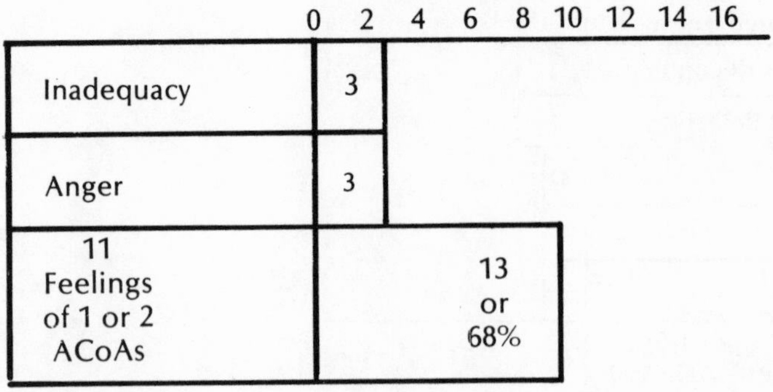

0 2 4 6 8 10 12 14 16

Inadequacy	3
Anger	3
11 Feelings of 1 or 2 ACoAs	13 or 68%

BREAKDOWN OF CONTROL DATA
BY AGE AND SEX

Doesn't Apply — 26/117 = 22%

	Female (15)	Male (11)
20-30	10	6
31-40	2	2
41-50	3	3
51+	0	0

No Bad Feeling — 5/117

	Female (8)	Male (7)
20-30	5	4
31-40	1	0
41-50	0	1
51+	2	2

Stress — 14/117

	Female (8)	Male (6)
20-30	6	3
31-40	1	0
41-50	0	0
51+	1	3

CONTROL-117
(National Random Sample)

BAD FEELINGS ON THE JOB

FEMALES			MALES	
AGE RANGE	AVERAGE		AGE RANGE	AVERAGE
20-30	35		20-30	24
30-40	11		30-40	6
40-50	16		40-50	3
50+	8		50+	8
TOTALS	**70**		**TOTALS**	**47**

FEELING #1 — Doesn't Apply (26/117) = 22%
Female (15/70) = 21%
Male (11/47) = 23%

FEELING #2 — No bad feeling (15/117) = 13%
Female (8/70) = 11%
Male (7/47) = 12%

FEELING #3 — Stress (14/117) = 12%
Female (8/70) = 11%
Male (6/47) = 12%

FEELING #4 — Lack of Recognition (5/117) = 4%
Female (4/70) = 6%
Male (1/70) = 2%

FEELING #5 — Unappreciated (5/117) = 4%
Female (5/70) = 7%
Male (0/47) = 0%

FEELING #6 — Inadequate (3/117) = 3%
Female (3/70) = 4%
Male (0/47) = 0%

BIBLIOGRAPHY

Beyer, Janice M., and Trice, Harrison M., *(See Trice below)*

Podolsky, Doug M., RTI Report: Economic Costs of Alcohol Abuse and Alcoholism. *Alcohol Health and Research World,* Winter 1984/ 1985, pp. 34-35.

Shealey, Tom: Your Secret Stress Signals. *Prevention Magazine,* September 1985, Vol. 37, No. 9, pp. 68-72.

Sonnenstuhl, William J.: Understanding EAP Self-referral: Toward a Social Network Approach. *Contemporary Drug Problems,* Summer 1982, pp. 269-293.

Steele, Paul D. and Hubbard, Robert L.: Management Styles, Perceptions of Substance Abuse and Employee Assistance Programs in Organizations. *The Journal of Applied Behavioral Science,* 1985, Vol. 21, No. 3, pp. 271-286.

Trice Harrison M.: Employee Assistance Programs: Where Do We Stand in 1983? *Journal of Psychiatric Treatment and Evaluation,* 1983, Vol. 5, pp. 521-552

Trice, Harrison M. and Beyer, Janice M.: A Databased Examination of Selection Bias in the Evaluation of Job-based Alcoholism Program. *Alcoholism: Clinical and Experimental Research,* Fall 1981, Vol. 5, No. 4, pp.489-496.

A Retrospective Study of Similarities and Differences Between Men and Women Employees in a Job-based Alcoholism Program: 1976-1977. *Journal of Drug Issues,* 1981, Vol. 11, pp. 233-262.

Employee Assistance Programs: Blending Performance — Oriented and Humanitarian Ideologies to Assist Emotionally Disturbed Employees. *Research in Community and Mental Health,* 1984, Vol. 4, pp. 245-259.

Work-Related Outcomes of the Constructive Confrontation Strategy in a Job-based Alcoholism Program. *Journal of Studies on Alcohol,* September 1984, Vol. 45, No. 5, pp. 393-404.